Working Memory Activities

A Workbook to Develop Memory Skills

David Newman

Speech-Language Pathologist

www.speechlanguage-resources.com

A Friendly Reminder

© David Newmonic Language Games 2013 - 2016

This book and all its contents are intellectual property.

All illustrations by David Newman

No part of this publication may be stored in a retrieval system, transmitted or reproduced in any way, including but not limited to digital copying and printing without the prior agreement and written permission of the author.

However, I do give permission for class teachers or speech-language pathologists to print and copy individual worksheets for student use. All pages in Appendix A are photocopiable

Working Memory

Activities

David Newman

Speech-Language Pathologist

www.speechlanguage-resources.com

ISBN: 13: 978-1492912682

Contents

What is Working Memory?... 6

Introduction and Organization 7

Tips on how to best use this book 9

Section 1 – Memory Test.. 11

Memory Test Form... 13

Section 2 – Digit Recall 15

Section 3 - Attributes.. 21

Section 4 – Working Memory Colours 29

House Drawing... 31

Farm Animal Drawing... 35

Train Drawing... 39

Section 5 – House furniture 45

House Plan and furniture.. 47

Section 6 – Working Memory Boxes 83

Working Memory Shapes 85

Working Memory Box 86

Section 7 – Working Memory Street Directions.............................. 121

Street Directions – Tutorial *Game Items*...................................... 120

Street Directions - Tutorial *Example*.. 123

Street Directions - Game Layout 127

Street Directions - Game items.. 132

References.. 166

Appendix A.. 167

Appendix B.. 179

About the Author 183

What is Working Memory?

Working memory is the ability of individuals to process and shape incoming auditory information in a short amount of time. A useful analogy to help explain working memory is to describe it as a mental note pad, similar in function to a post-it note, where a message is mentally jotted down to be used quickly.

Working memory requires the ability to store information just long enough to work or manipulate it before it *vanishes*. Children with poor working memory struggle to retain new information long enough to process it accurately. If the new information cannot be processed quickly, it soon becomes lost.

An example of working memory in action is the simple task of memorizing a list of animals, in this instance the animals are *horse*, *dog,* and *rhinoceros*. To remember the three different animal species requires us to use our mental storage capacity which is not too difficult a task. A more difficult exercise is to sort the animals ranging from the *heaviest* animal to the *lightest*. It's the mental working out and sorting of the heaviest animal *(rhinoceros)* down to the lightest animal *(dog)* that is mentally taxing. Within the context of a school classroom, it is this working or *manipulation* of recently heard information that many students find difficult to perform.

The Organization of the Working Memory Activities Book

The working memory activities in this book are divided into sections. Each section features challenging exercises designed to prod students to use their memory systems. Students are prompted to mentally arrange and organize information in their working memory before performing a complex task. *The tasks in this book are best suited for students between the ages 7 to 12.*

The activities are divided into eight sections:

Working Memory Test: This test is an informal way of gathering a pre - intervention understanding of a student's ability with digit recall. The test features a *pre-test - post-test* form which provides both a baseline and a means of gauging a student's progress after completing the many working memory tasks.

Digit Recall: These tasks progress from easy to difficult. Students are required to repeat numbers, both forward and backward. Repeating numbers backward stimulates working memory resources and has the potential to stimulate memory skills.

Word Sequence – Attributes: Students are required to mentally arrange familiar animals and objects such as from smallest to largest. These activities prompt students to use their working memory abilities just long enough to place the objects into a logical order.

Working Memory – Colours: This section requires students to listen to an increasingly complex sequence of instructions and then colour in with coloured pencils a small subsection of a drawing. The *colours* activity is divided into **entry** level, **intermediate** level and **advanced** level.

Working Memory – Home Furniture: This section requires students to mentally arrange and place furniture items within the walls of a top-down view a house. The *home furniture* activity is divided into **entry** level, **intermediate** level and **advanced** level.

Working Memory – Shape Boxes: This section requires students to move several common shapes in different orientations within the confines of a rectangular box. The *shape boxes* activity is divided into **entry** level, **intermediate** level and **advanced** level.

Working Memory – Street Directions: This section requires students to move a car or motorbike along city streets and freeways to reach a destination. The street directions activity features detailed instruction on how to use the various game items such as a compass, custom ruler and left/right marker (all supplied) to successfully orient the vehicle to the correct destination. The *street directions* activity is divided into **entry** level, **intermediate** level and **advanced** level.

Appendix: *Appendix A* features photocopiable resources for all the different activities in the book, while *Appendix B* features answers for the **digit recall** and the **attributes** sections.

Tips on How to Best Use This Book

This book features many practical activities that will require some initial preparation.

- In appendix A there are a number of game-boards and items for each part which will need to be printed (or photocopied), cut out and laminated for parts 5 *(home furniture)* part 6 *(shape boxes)* and part 7 *(street directions)*.
- Parts 4 through to 7 each feature three stages for students to work through. The stages are *entry level*, *intermediate level* and *advanced level*.
- **Entry** level activities feature simple instructions and usually a one stage command.
- **Intermediate** level questions may feature more complex instructions and 2 to 3 stage commands.
- **Advanced** level questions primarily feature 2 to 4 stage commands with complex and highly detailed questions.
- It's recommended younger students (ages 7-8) complete the entry level questions several times and have a strong knowledge of the rules and mechanics of the particular activity before attempting the intermediate and advanced level activities. This is to ensure that the complexity of the intermediate and advanced level instructions don't confuse and/or overwhelm younger students' memory

capacities. *Record students' progress on the record sheet provided for each level.*

- The *home furniture* section features furniture items that are presented with a top-down view which may be confusing to younger students. Students will require some understanding of concepts **left/right** and **top/bottom**. Discuss the items with students and point to the distinguishing features of the various items, i.e. '*Do you have a /cooktop/fridge, sofa in your house?', 'in which room would you find a fridge?*' etc.

- The *street directions* section is perhaps the most complex and difficult unit to master. The activity features many separate components that must be coordinated by students before they can respond to the various activities in the entry, intermediate and advanced levels.

The *street directions* activity targets **working memory** abilities but also requires **organisational skills** and **critical thinking** abilities. It is recommended that students be guided through the instructions in some detail and learn to use components such as the *left/right marker*, the *custom ruler* and the *compass* before attempting the activities themselves. There are detailed instructions for all of the *street directions* components in **section 7**'s introduction.

Section 1

Memory Test

Memory Test

This memory test provides an informal measure of a student's memory ability. The results of the test can be used to establish a baseline. The baseline provides a means of measuring gains a student may make following a period of intervention. The baseline score can be compared to a retest score performed several weeks or months later.

Test Instructions: Inform the student that you are going to read a series of numbers that he/she has to repeat back to you in the correct sequence. Make certain that the student cannot see the digit sequences and then read the digits in a clear, slow and measured voice. Explain at the beginning of the test that you can only read the sequence *once*.

For each correct sequence score 1 point, for an incomplete or incorrect sequence score a 0. **If a student is incorrect with two consecutive test items within the same number of sequenced digits, discontinue the test.**

The test is in two parts. In **part 1** the student repeats digits *forwards*. For instance, **Clinician:** '*say these numbers*, 5 9 2 3.' The student is required to respond with the exact same sequence, **Student:** '5 9 2 3.' In **part 2** the student is required to repeat the digits *backwards*. For instance, **Clinician:** 'say these numbers backwards, 5 8 2.' The student is required to respond with 2 8 5.

Please note, repeating digits *backward* is a far more demanding and taxing task than repeating digits *forward*.

Working Memory Activities

Memory Test – Part 1

Student Name: _____   Date of Birth: _____

Date: *Pre-Test* : _____   Date: *Post-Test:* _____

Instructions: I am going to read a short sequence of numbers. You have to repeat the numbers back to me. So if I say 7 3, you say 7 3. I can only say the numbers once, so listen carefully.

Part 1 – Digits *Forwards*

Digits:	Pre-test	Post-test
4 8	_____	_____
6 3	_____	_____
9 7	_____	_____
8 5	_____	_____

Digits:	Pre-test	Post-test
6 9 2	_____	_____
4 7 3	_____	_____
9 5 1	_____	_____
8 3 9	_____	_____

Digits:	Pre-test	Post-test
6 1 4 5	_____	_____
4 3 8 1	_____	_____
9 8 1 4	_____	_____
8 7 1 9	_____	_____

Digits:	Pre-test	Post-test
9 3 1 8 7	_____	_____
1 7 2 4 8	_____	_____
6 3 1 2 1	_____	_____
1 3 9 6 8	_____	_____

Memory Test – Part 2

Instructions: I am going to read a short sequence of numbers. You have to repeat the numbers back to me, but this time it's a little different. I want you to say the numbers *backwards*. So if I say 7 3, you say 3 7. I can only say the numbers once, so listen carefully.

Part 2 – Digits *Backwards*

Digits:		Pre-test	Post-test
3 9	*(9 3)*	_____	_____
6 3	*(3 6)*	_____	_____
9 7	*(7 9)*	_____	_____
8 5	*(5 8)*	_____	_____

Digits:		Pre-test	Post-test
2 9 4	*(4 9 2)*	_____	_____
4 7 3	*(3 7 4)*	_____	_____
8 5 4	*(4 5 8)*	_____	_____
7 3 1	*(1 3 7)*	_____	_____

Digits:		Pre-test	Post-test
9 1 2 8	*(8 2 1 9)*	_____	_____
4 1 5 9	*(9 5 1 4)*	_____	_____
3 7 1 2	*(2 1 7 3)*	_____	_____
2 8 7 1	*(1 7 8 2)*	_____	_____

Digits:		Pre-test	Post-test
6 3 1 8 1	*(1 8 1 3 6)*	_____	_____
7 3 2 4 9	*(9 4 2 3 7)*	_____	_____
1 3 4 2 7	*(7 2 4 3 1)*	_____	_____
4 3 7 6 2	*(2 6 7 3 4)*	_____	_____

Section 2

Digit Recall

Working Memory-Digit Recall

Digit Recall (2 digits)

Instructions: I'm going to read out some numbers. I want you to listen carefully and then repeat the same numbers back to me.

2 – 5

4 – 9

7 – 3

2 – 5

6 – 9

Instructions: I'm going to read out some more numbers. But this time it's a bit different. I want you to listen carefully and then repeat the same numbers back to me, but backwards. So if I say 2 – 8, you say 8 – 2.

7 – 2   (2 – 7)

3 – 1   (1 – 3)

2 – 8   (8 – 2)

5 – 1   (1 – 5)

2 – 6   (6 – 2)

Digit Recall (3 digits)

Instructions: I'm going to read out some numbers. I want you to listen carefully and then repeat the same numbers back to me.

8 – 5 – 6

5 – 9 – 4

9 – 1 – 7

9 – 1 – 2

7 – 3 – 1

Instructions: I'm going to read out some more numbers. But this time it's a bit different. I want you to listen carefully and then repeat the same numbers to me, but backwards. So if I say 2 – 8 - 3, you say 3 - 8 – 2.

2 – 8 – 1   (1 – 8 – 2)

5 – 2 – 4   (4 – 2 – 5)

8 – 4 – 2   (2 – 4 – 8)

1 – 9 – 6   (6 – 9 – 1)

9 – 7 – 4   (4 – 7 – 9)

Digit Recall (4 digits)

Instructions: I'm going to read out some numbers. I want you to listen carefully and then repeat the same numbers back to me.

6 – 3 – 9 – 1

1 – 4 - 8 – 9

8 – 4 - 9 - 1

4 – 6 – 1 - 9

7 – 1 – 8 – 3

Instructions: I'm going to read out some more numbers. But this time it's a bit different. I want you to listen carefully and then repeat the same numbers to me, but backwards. So if I say 2 – 8 – 3 - 7, you say 7 - 3 - 8 – 2.

3 – 4 – 9 – 8   (8 – 9 – 4 - 3)

6 – 1 – 8 – 2   (2 – 8 – 1 – 6)

5 – 3 – 6 – 2   (2 – 6 – 3 – 5)

6 – 4 – 6 – 1   (1 – 6 – 4 – 6)

1 – 6 – 7 – 2   (2 – 7 – 6 – 1)

Digit Recall (5 digits)

Instructions: I'm going to read out some numbers. I want you to listen carefully and then repeat the same numbers back to me.

7 – 2 – 9 – 4 - 5

8 – 1 - 2 – 0 - 3

2 – 4 - 7 – 1 - 8

3 – 6 – 1 – 7 - 1

1 – 9 – 8 – 3 - 5

Digit Recall (6 digits)

Instructions: I'm going to read out some numbers. I want you to listen carefully and then repeat the same numbers back to me.

7 – 3 – 9 – 1 – 2 - 7

9 – 4 - 8 – 9 – 5 - 6

3 – 4 - 9 – 1 – 8 - 2

1 – 6 – 1 – 9 – 2 - 9

9 – 1 – 8 – 3 – 1 – 8

Section 3

Attributes

Attributes

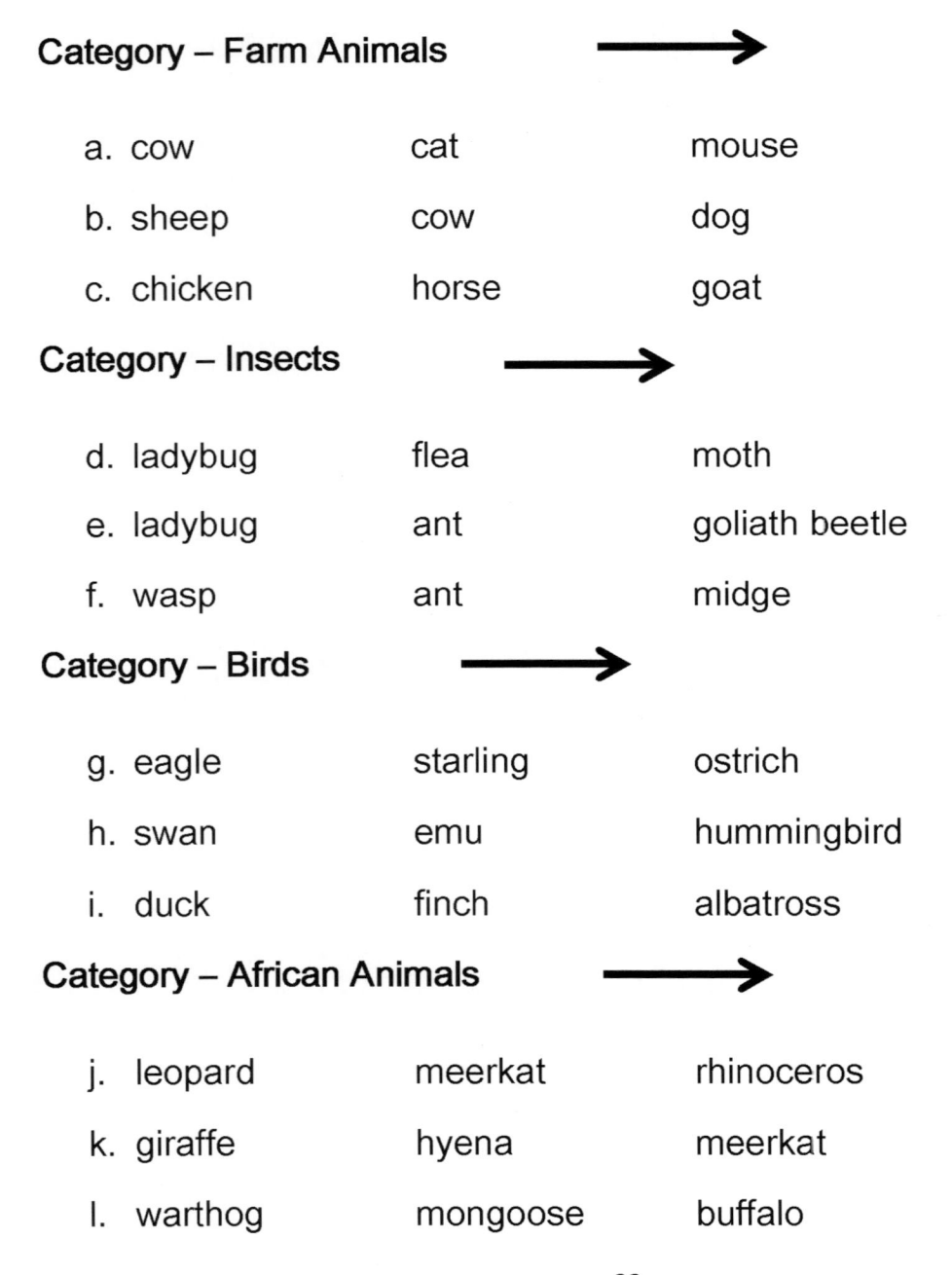

Word Sequence–physical attributes

Instructions: I'm going to read out a list of animals to you. I want you to listen carefully and then say them in order from **smallest** to **largest**. So for instance if I was to say **cat, ant, cow** you would say *ant, cat, cow.*

Smallest to Largest

Category – Farm Animals ⟶

    a. cow   cat   mouse
    b. sheep   cow   dog
    c. chicken   horse   goat

Category – Insects ⟶

    d. ladybug   flea   moth
    e. ladybug   ant   goliath beetle
    f. wasp   ant   midge

Category – Birds ⟶

    g. eagle   starling   ostrich
    h. swan   emu   hummingbird
    i. duck   finch   albatross

Category – African Animals ⟶

    j. leopard   meerkat   rhinoceros
    k. giraffe   hyena   meerkat
    l. warthog   mongoose   buffalo

Word Sequence–physical attributes

Instructions: I'm going to read out a list of foods to you. I want you to listen carefully and then say them in order from smallest to largest. So for instance if I was to say *grape, watermelon, apple* you would say *grape, apple, watermelon*.

Smallest to Largest

Category – Fruits

    a. orange   cherry   grapefruit ⟶

    b. grape   watermelon   apple

    c. lemon   plum   watermelon

Category – Vegetables ⟶

    d. cabbage   bean   zucchini

    e. capsicum   pumpkin   bean

    f. sweet potato   eggplant   peas

Category – Nuts & Seeds ⟶

    g. peanut   brazil nut   macadamia nut

    h. chestnut   almond   sesame seed

    i. walnut   pumpkin seed   peanut

Attributes

Word Sequence–physical attributes

Instructions: I'm going to read out a list of objects to you. I want you to listen carefully and then say them in order from **longest** to **shortest and tallest** to **shortest**. So for instance if I was to say *pen, nail, ruler* you would say, *ruler, pen, nail*.

Longest to Shortest →

a. ruler finger pen
b. train motorbike truck
c. baseball bat paper clip spanner

d. tree twig branch
e. pond river lake
f. sardine barracouta shark

Shortest to Tallest →

a. St Bernard Spaniel Chihuahua
b. Gorilla  baboon
c. lion Giraffe meerkat

d. hill mountain hillock
e. shed tower dollhouse
f. weed tree shrub

Word Sequence–physical attributes

Instructions: I'm going to read out a list of objects to you. I want you to listen carefully and then say them in order from **heaviest** to **lightest**. So for instance if I was to say tissue, *frying pan, apple* you would say, *frying pan, apple, tissue*.

Heaviest to Lightest ⟶

a.	medicine ball	tennis ball	football
b.	golf ball	basketball	baseball
c.	broom	toothbrush	street sweeper
d.	dinghy	aircraft carrier	motorboat
e.	scooter	motorbike	truck
f.	ultra-light	passenger jet	helicopter
g.	flea	moth	hawk
h.	elephant	mouse	dog
i.	canary	ostrich	hawk
j.	watch	flat screen TV	laptop
k.	book	computer	pen
l.	glass	frypan	oven

Attributes

Word Sequence–physical attributes

Instructions: I'm going to read out a list of objects to you. I want you to listen carefully and then say them in order from **thickest** to **thinnest**. So for instance if I was to say *pencil, brick, mobile phone* you would say, *brick, mobile phone, pencil.*

Thickest to Thinnest ⟶

a. pin — brick — sausage
b. card — encyclopaedia — newspaper
c. rope — thread — cable

d. bean — pin — log
e. finger — leg — single hair
f. branch — pin — tree trunk

g. praying mantis — hippopotamus — goat
h. car tire — dinner plate — cake
i. paper — loaf of bread — CD cover

j. arrow — harpoon — rocket ship
k. nail — tree — pin
l. DVD — cake — car tire

Working Memory Activities

Word Sequence–physical attributes

Instructions: I'm going to read out a list of objects to you. I want you to listen carefully and then say them in order from **coldest** to **warmest**. So for instance if I was to say *hot potato, ice cube, banana*, you would say, *ice cube, banana, hot potato*.

Coldest to Warmest

a. desert	snow	rainforest
b. Sahara	Antarctica	beach in Australia
c. Autumn/Fall	Summer	Winter
d. apple	hot chocolate	ice cube
e. frozen peas	hot pie	apple
f. honey	hot soup	icy pole
g. hot tub	snow field	hall
h. snow field	forest	erupting volcano
i. water from fridge	hot chocolate	tap water
j. Arctic ocean	lake	hot springs
k. snow	desert sand	lava
l. hot springs	lava	tap water

Section 4

Colours

Important: Please note that for *all responses* students may not begin the activity until the clinician has <u>completed</u> the directions.

Working Memory – Colours

Instructions

The activities in this section prompt children to colour in a house to a pre-set range of oral questions.

You will need...

- Photocopied sheets of the house picture
- Coloured pencils
- A pair of scissors

***Photocopy** multiple copies of the house before you begin.* Read the **directions** to the child in a clear voice and at a slow rate. Some children, depending on their abilities, may require the questions to be repeated.

After each activity is completed, repeat the instructions while the student checks their responses. If a child has some difficulty with the *entry* level activities, redo the *entry* level activity and provide extra scaffolding for the child as needed before venturing on to the *Intermediate* level. You will need a **fresh photocopied** sheet for each level of each activity.

House Drawing *Photocopiable*

Working Memory – Colours

Entry Level

Activity 1

1. Colour the left front window with a green pencil.
2. Colour the tall tree yellow.
3. Colour the front of the chimney blue.
4. Colour the middle mountain brown.
5. Colour the left front door red.
6. Colour the side of the chimney green.
7. Colour the top window on the side of the house yellow.
8. Colour the roof of the rear shed blue.

Working Memory – Colours

Intermediate Level

Activity 2

1. Colour the left mountain blue and the window on the rear shed red.

2. Colour the short triangular tree orange and the right front door green.

3. Colour the lower left side window blue and the top of the chimney grey.

4. Colour the roof to the left of the chimney grey and the roof to the right of the chimney orange.

5. Colour the top of the right mountain purple and thebush to the left of the house yellow.

Working Memory – Colours

Advanced Level

Activity 3

1. Colour the base of mountain to the right orange and then colour the bush closest to the tall tree purple.

2. After colouring the base of the tall triangular tree green, colour the lower side window on the far right blue.

3. Before you colour the top of the middle mountain red, colour the front right window blue.

4. Circle the chimney with a blue pencil after you circle the left front door green.

5. Colour the base of the trees to the left of the house green and then colour the path that leads to the house yellow.

Farm Animals Drawing *Photocopiable*

Working Memory – Colours

Entry Level

Activity 4

1. Colour the cow's ears brown.
2. Colour the cow's nose black.
3. Colour the horse's tail green.
4. Colour the horse's mane yellow.
5. Colour the cow's hooves red.
6. Colour the horse's two front legs orange.
7. Colour the cow's horns green.
8. Colorr the cow's tail yellow.

Working Memory – Colours

Intermediate Level

Activity 5

1. Colour the horse's tail blue and the cow's left ear yellow.
2. Colour the cow's left back leg orange and the cow's right horn green.
3. Colour the horse's head brown, the horse's back legs orange and the cow's tail blue.
4. Colour the horse's hooves green, the cow's front legs brown and the horse's ears yellow.
5. Colour the horse's mane green, the cow's right ear red and the cow's left eye blue.

Working Memory – Colours

Advanced Level

Activity 6

1. Colour the cow's udder orange before you colour the horse's head orange.

2. After colouring the horse's front legs brown, colour the cow's left ear red.

3. Before you colour the cow's hooves green, colour the horse's hooves orange.

4. Colour the cow's nose yellow after you colour the horse's tail blue.

5. Colour the cow's nose red and then circle the two front legs of the horse with a blue pencil.

Train and Carriage Drawing *Photocopiable*

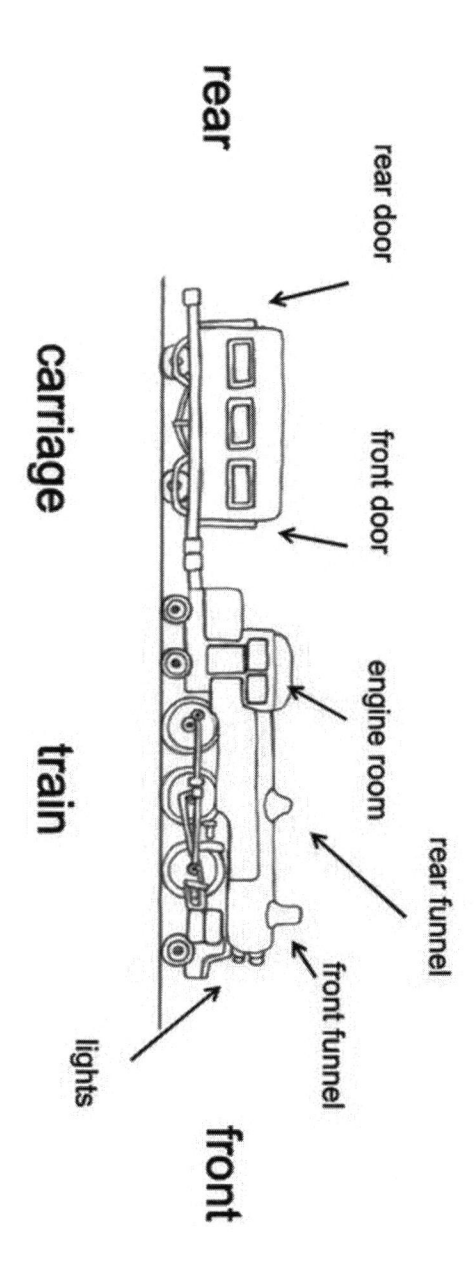

rear

rear door

carriage

front door

engine room

train

rear funnel

front funnel

lights

front

Train and Carriage Drawing *Photocopiable*

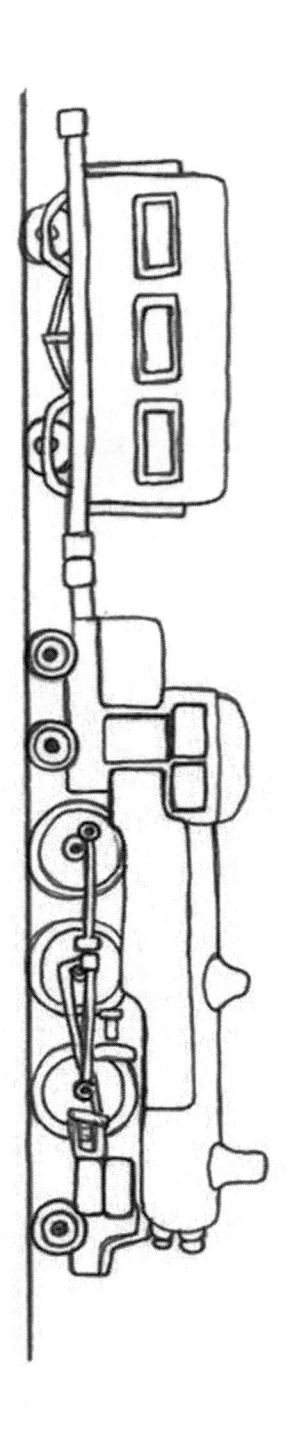

Working Memory – Colours

Entry Level

Activity 7

1. Colour the carriage red.
2. Colour the train green.
3. Colour the rear door of the carriage blue.
4. Colour the small front wheel of the train yellow.
5. Colour the rear small wheel of the train green.
6. Colour the middle window of the carriage orange.
7. Colour the rear wheel of the carriage black.
8. Colour the large center wheel of the train blue.

Working Memory – Colours

Intermediate Level

Activity 8

1. Colour the front funnel blue and the rear funnel grey.
2. Colour the front window of the carriage green and the large right wheel of the train orange.
3. Colour the two small rear wheels of the train blue and the small front wheel of the carriage yellow.
4. Colour the engine room windows yellow and the rear window of the carriage purple.
5. Colour the left large wheel of the train purple, and the rear wheel of the carriage black.

Working Memory – Colours

Advanced Level

Activity 9

1. Colour the middle window of the carriage blue, the front wheel of the carriage yellow and thefront door of the carriage red.

2. After colouring the bottom of the train light grey, colour the two small rear wheels of the train black.

3. Before you colour the front funnel grey, colour the rear funnel blue.

4. Colour all the train's large wheels green except the middle wheel, which is to be coloured blue.

5. Colour the rear door of the carriage purple after you colour the front lights of the train blue.

Working Memory – Colours

Record Sheet

Tick √ for correct and ✗ for incorrect

House

1. Activity   __ __ __ __ __ __ __ __
2. Activty   __ __ __ __ __
3. Activity   __ __ __ __ __

Farm Animals

4. Activity   __ __ __ __ __
5. Activity   __ __ __ __ __
6. Activity   __ __ __ __ __

Train

7. Activity   __ __ __ __ __ __ __ __
8. Activity   __ __ __ __ __
9. Activity   __ __ __ __ __

Section 5

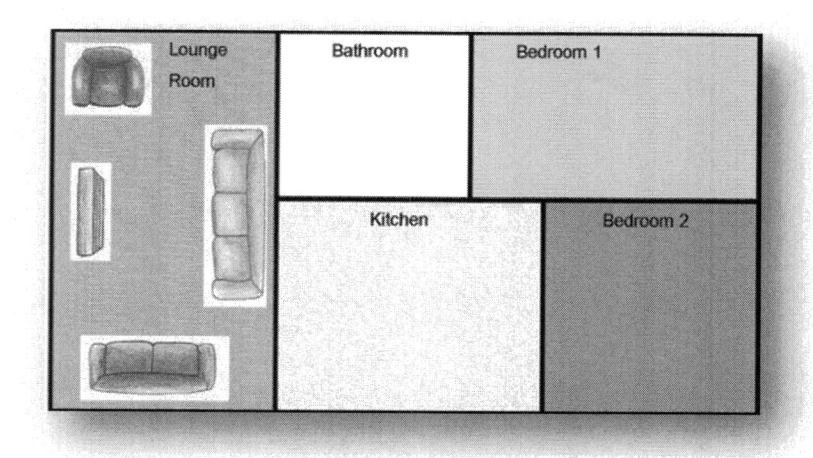

Home Furniture

Important: Please note that for *all responses* students may not begin the activity until the clinician has <u>completed</u> the directions.

Working Memory – Home Furniture

Instructions

The activities in this section prompt children to move furniture items within the confines of a house plan. Encourage students to use the left/right marker from section 7 if they have difficulty with the **left v right** concept.

You will need...

- A photocopied sheet of the furniture drawings
- A photocopied sheet of the house box
- A pair of scissors
- A laminator (optional)

Cut out and laminate the furniture items and the house plan. Present all the furniture items and the top down view of the house interior to students, explaining what each area of the house is and to think of what types of furniture may go in each room. Explain to students that they have been tasked with *positioning* furniture within the house and need to follow directions carefully and exactly.

If students have some difficulty with the *entry* level activities, redo the *entry* level section and provide extra scaffolding for students as needed before moving on to the *Intermediate* level.

Working Memory Activities

	Lounge Room
Kitchen	Bathroom
Bedroom 2	Bedroom 1

House Plan & Furniture - *Photocopiable*

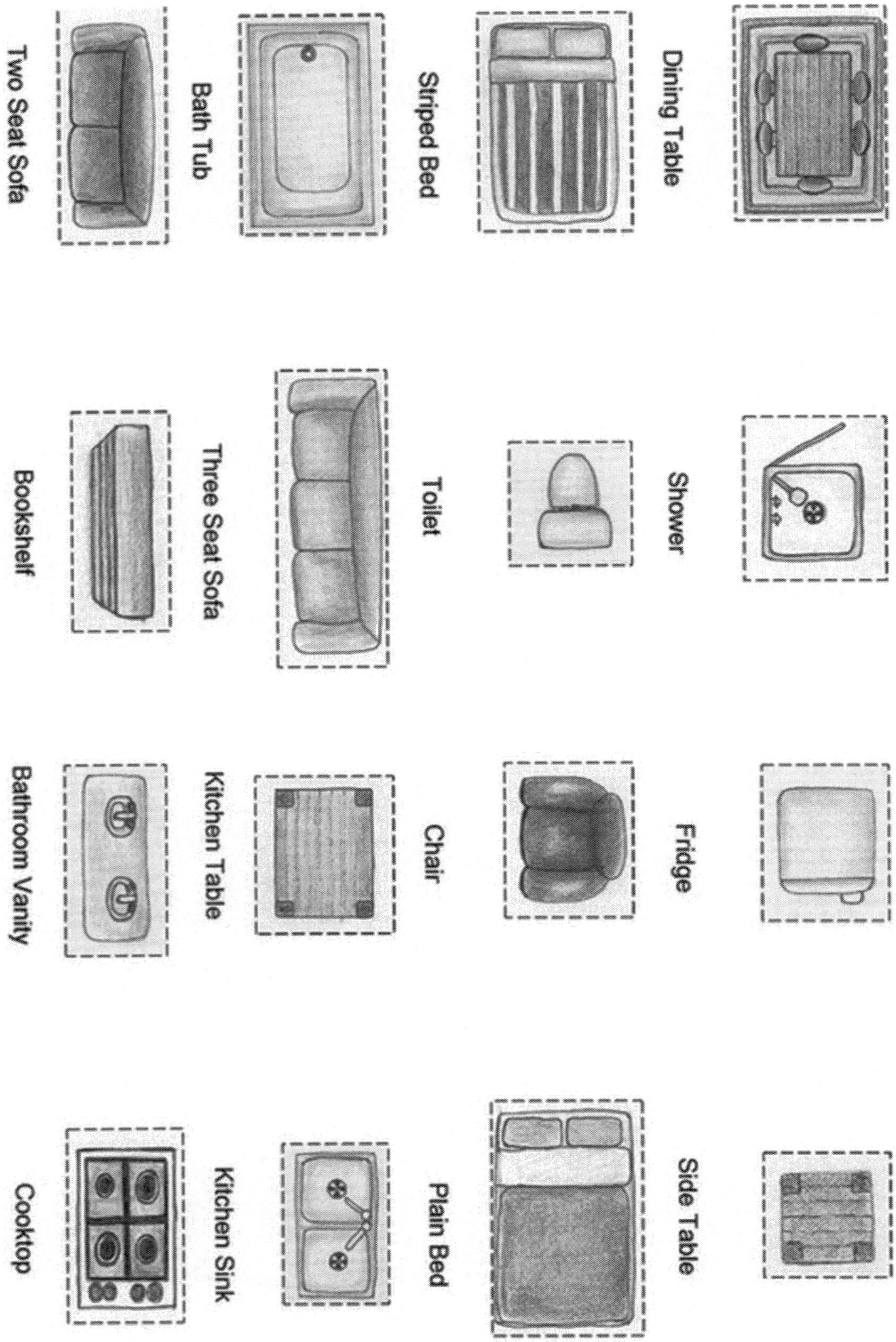

- Two Seat Sofa
- Bath Tub
- Striped Bed
- Dining Table
- Bookshelf
- Three Seat Sofa
- Toilet
- Shower
- Sink
- Bathroom Vanity
- Kitchen Table
- Chair
- Fridge
- Cooktop
- Kitchen Sink
- Plain Bed
- Side Table

Working Memory – Home Furniture

Entry Level

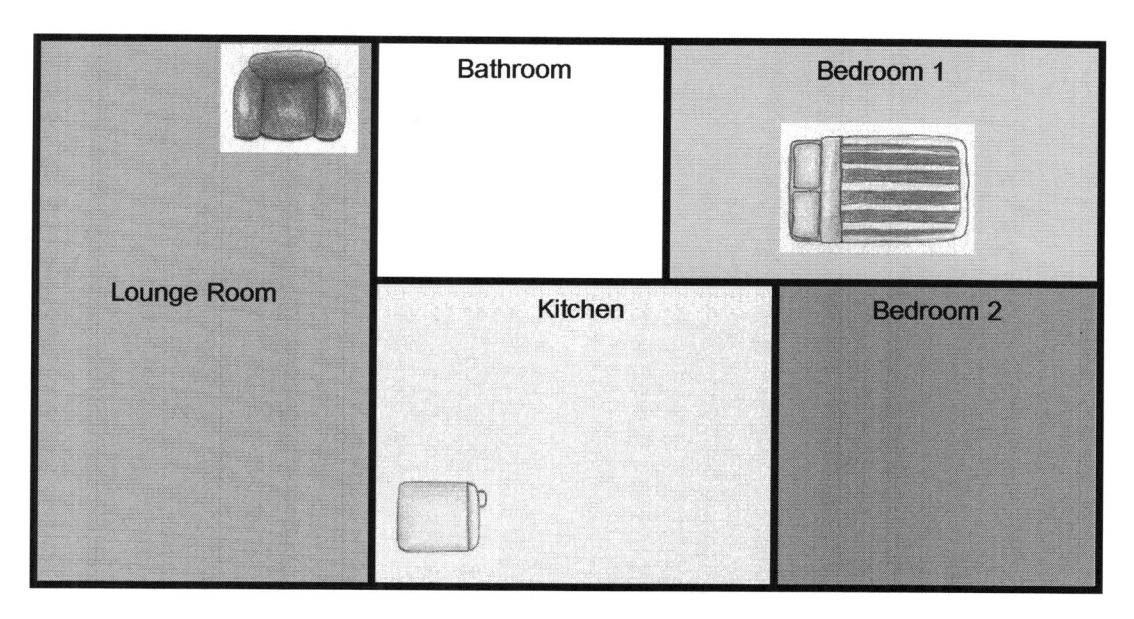

Activity 1

1. Select the fridge, the striped bed and the chair.
2. Place the fridge in the bottom left corner of the kitchen.
3. Place the striped bed in the middle of bedroom 1.
4. Place the chair in the top right corner of the lounge room.

Working Memory – Home Furniture

Entry Level

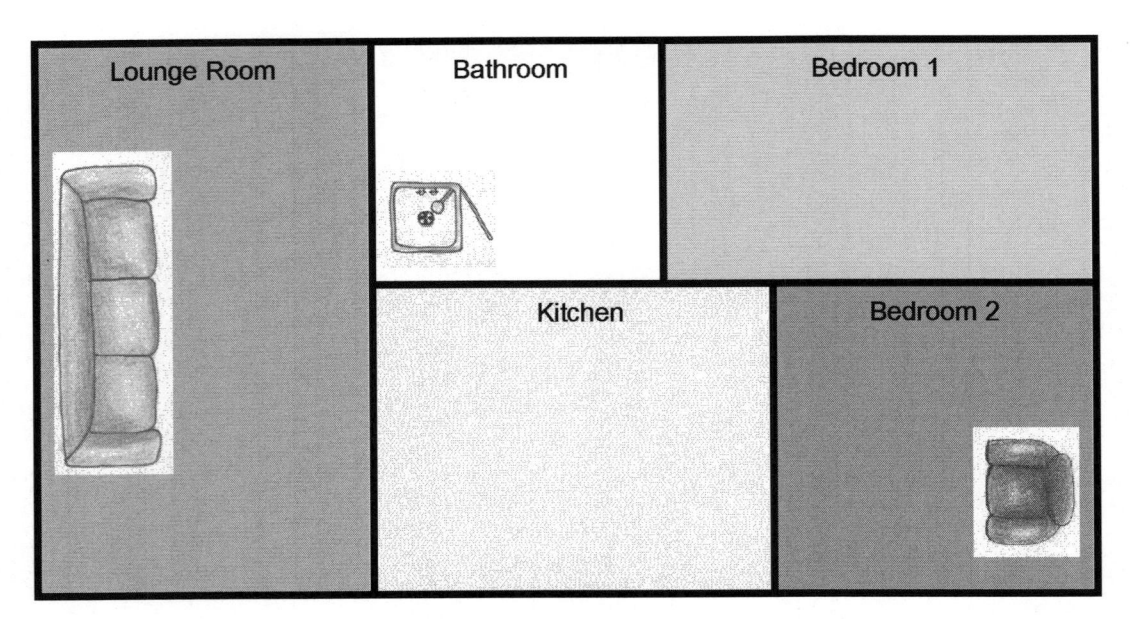

Activity 2

1. Select the three seat sofa, the shower and the chair.
2. Place the chair in the bottom right corner of bedroom 2.
3. Place the shower in the bottom left corner of the bathroom.
4. Place the three seat sofa along the left wall of the loungeroom.

Working Memory – Home Furniture

Entry Level

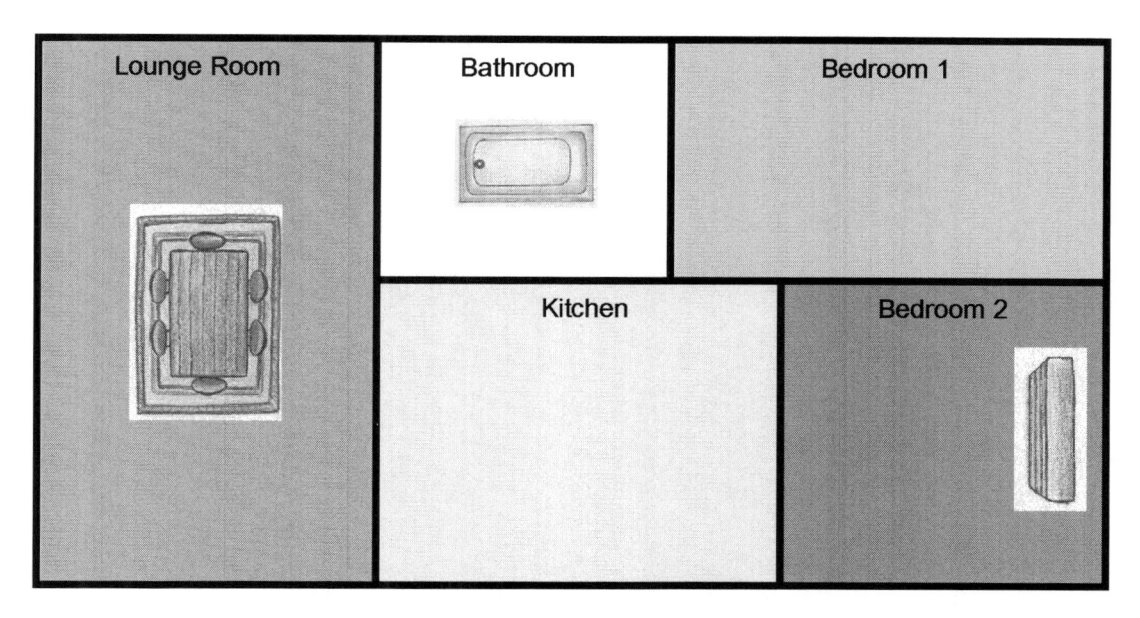

Lounge Room	Bathroom	Bedroom 1
	Kitchen	Bedroom 2

Activity 3

1. Select the dining table, the bath and the bookcase.
2. Place the dining table in the middle of the lounge room.
3. Place the bath lengthways in the middle of the bathroom.
4. Place the bookshelf along the right wall of bedroom 2.

Working Memory – Home Furniture

Entry Level

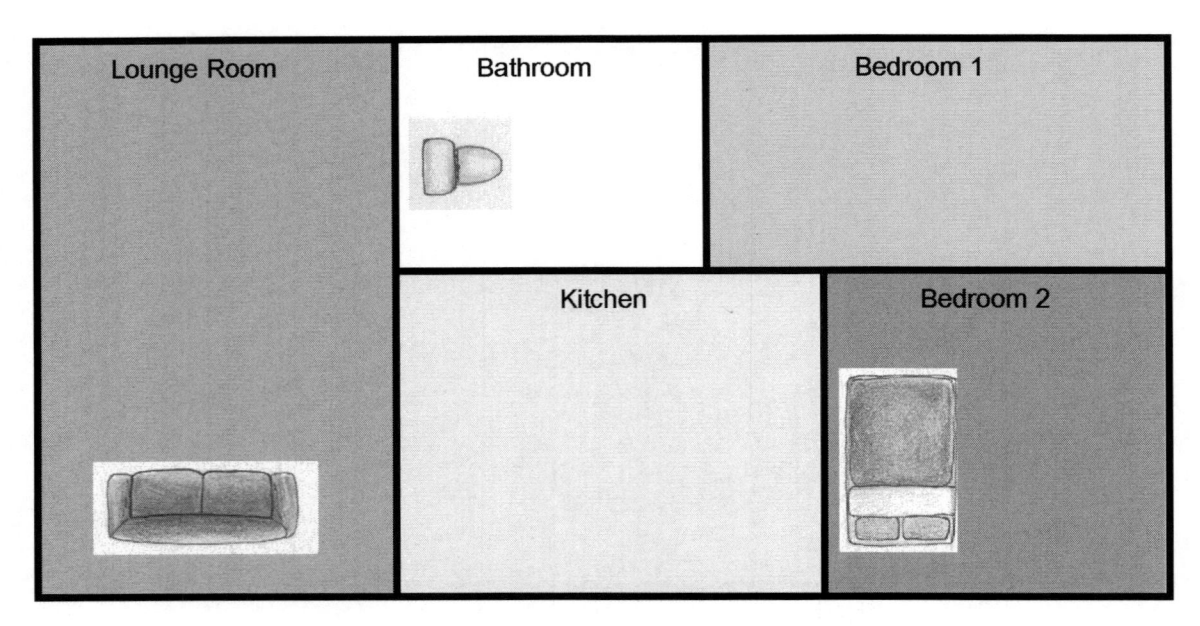

Activity 4

1. Select the two seat sofa, the toilet and the plain bed.
2. Place the toilet along the left wall of the bathroom.
3. Place the two seat sofa along the bottom wall of the lounge room.
4. Place the plain bed along the left wall of bedroom 2.

Working Memory – Home Furniture

Entry Level

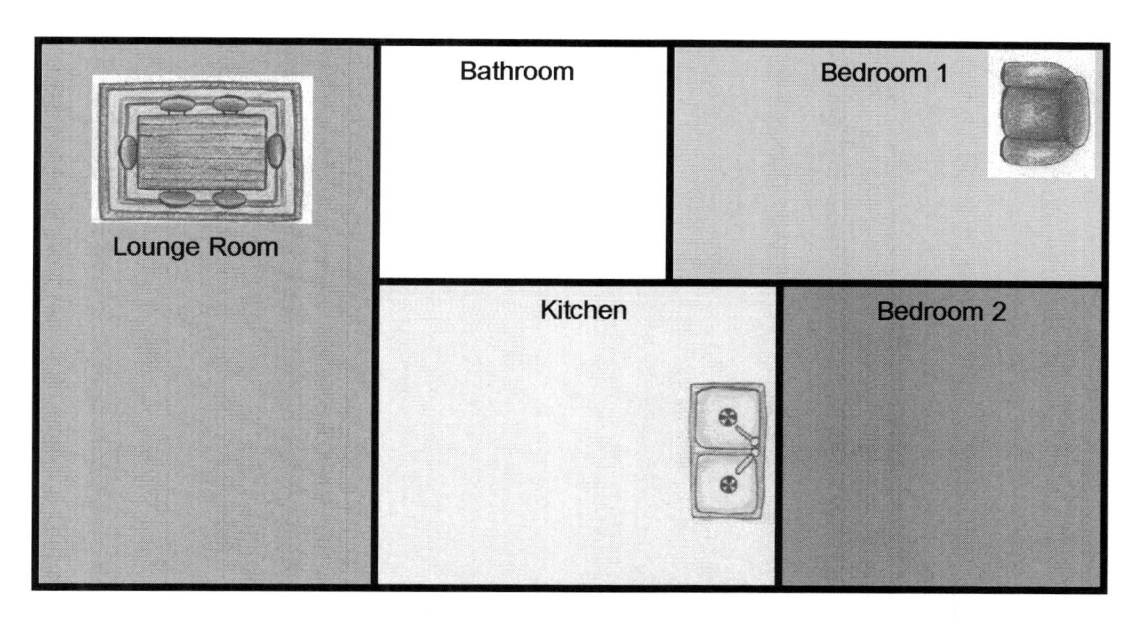

Activity 5

1. Select the dining table, the kitchen sink and the chair.

2. Place the dining table along the top wall in the lounge room.

3. Place the kitchen sink along the right wall in the kitchen.

4. Place the chair in the top right corner of bedroom 1.

Working Memory – Home Furniture

Entry Level

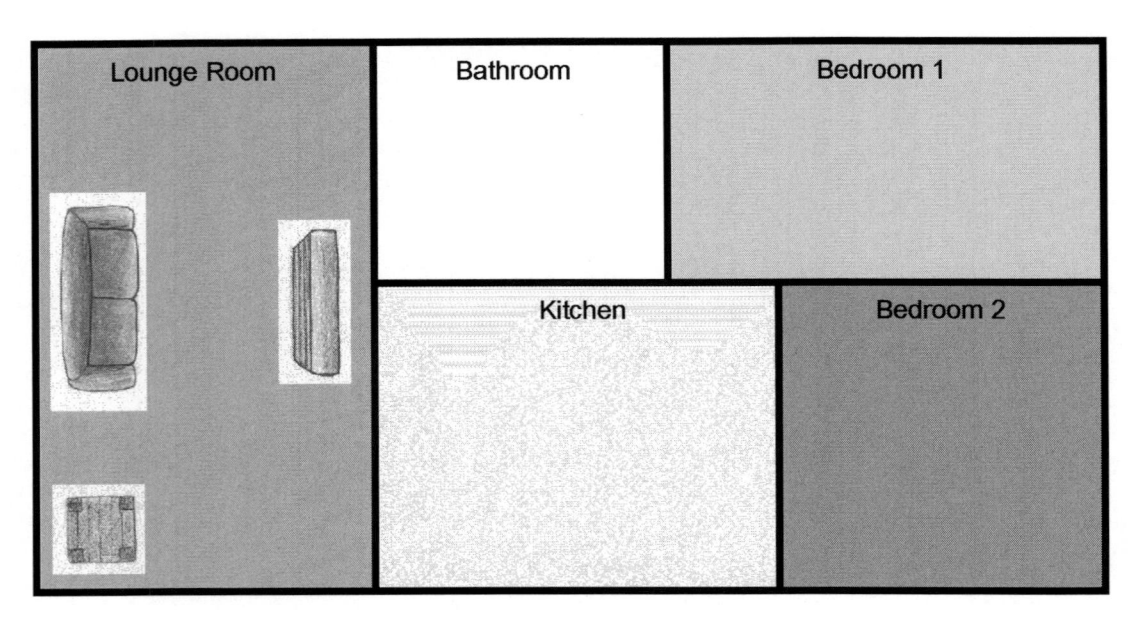

Activity 6

1. Select the two seat sofa, the side table and the bookshelf.
2. Place the two seat sofa half way up the left wall of the lounge room.
3. Place the side table in the bottom left corner of the lounge room.
4. Place the bookshelf directly opposite the two seat sofa.

Working Memory – Home Furniture

Entry Level

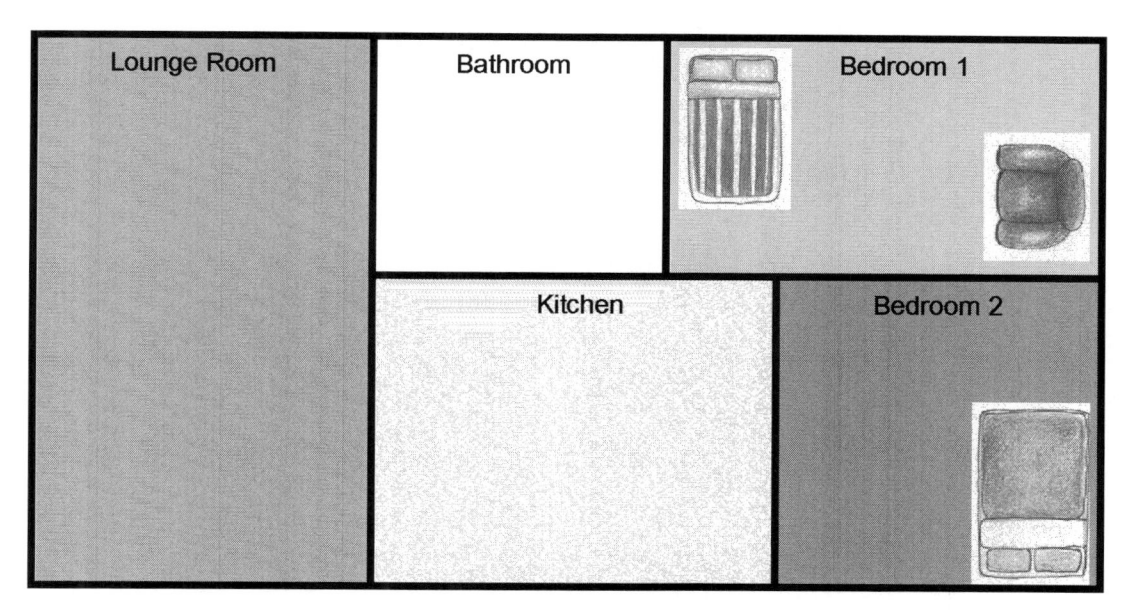

Activity 7

1. Select the striped bed, the plain bed and the chair.
2. Place the striped bed in the top left corner of bedroom 1 with the pillows facing near the top wall.
3. Place the chair in the bottom right corner of bedroom 1.
4. Place the plain bed in the bottom right corner of bedroom 2 with the pillows facing near the bottom wall.

Working Memory – Home Furniture

Entry Level

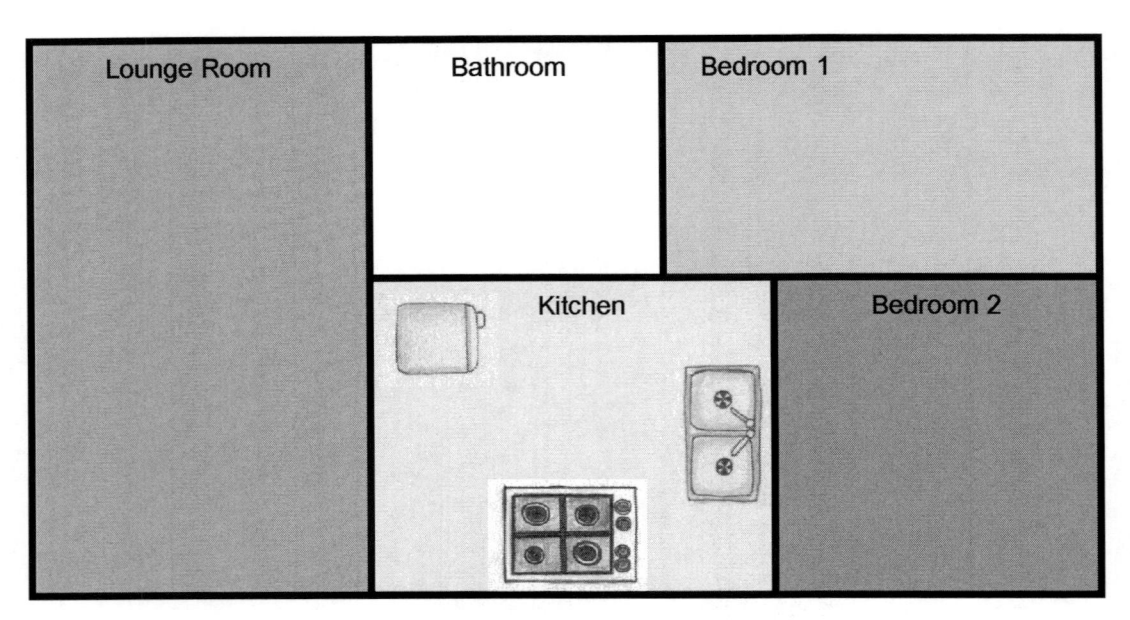

Activity 8

1. Select the kitchen sink, the fridge and the cooktop.

2. Place the cooktop on the bottom wall of the kitchen.

3. Place the kitchen sink along the right wall of the kitchen.

4. Place the fridge in the top left corner of the kitchen.

Working Memory – Home Furniture

Entry Level

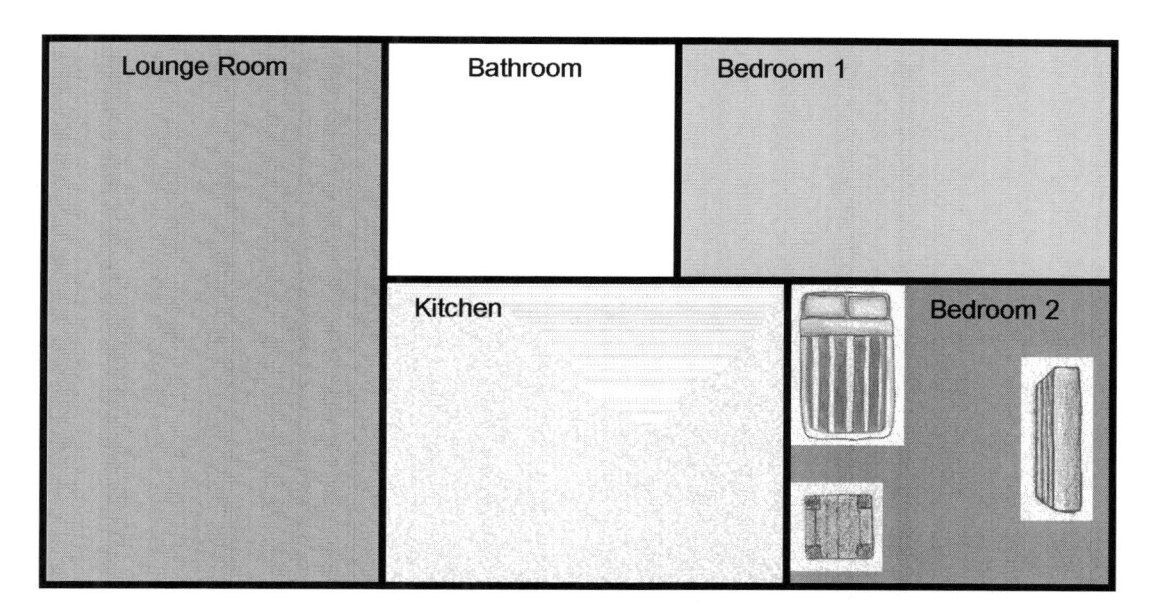

Activity 9

1. Select the striped bed, the bookshelf and the side table.

2. Place the striped bed in the top left corner of bedroom 2.

3. Place the side table in the bottom left corner of bedroom 2.

4. Place the bookshelf along the right wall of bedroom 2.

Working Memory – Home Furniture

Entry Level

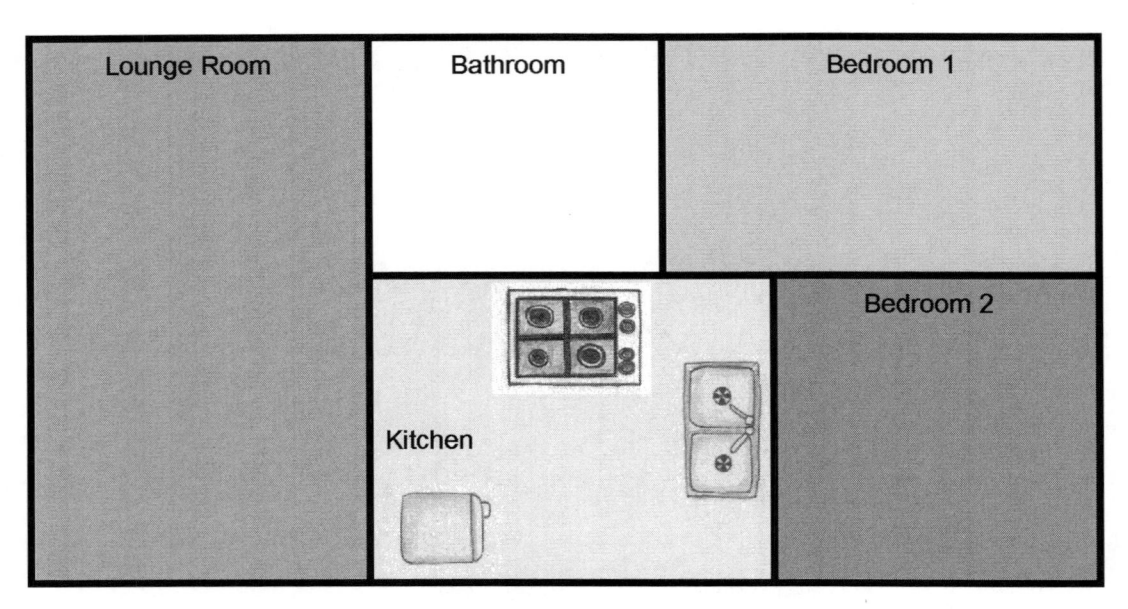

Activity 10

1. Select the cooktop, the kitchen sink and the fridge.
2. Place the cooktop along the top wall of the kitchen in the middle.
3. Place the fridge in the bottom left corner of the kitchen.
4. Place the kitchen sink along the right wall of the kitchen in the middle.

Working Memory - Furniture

Record Sheet

Tick √ for correct and ✗ for incorrect

Entry Level

Activity 1 __ __ __ __   Activity 6 __ __ __ __

Activty 2 __ __ __ __   Activity 7 __ __ __ __

Activity 3 __ __ __ __   Activity 8 __ __ __ __

Activity 4 __ __ __ __   Activity 9 __ __ __ __

Activity 5 __ __ __ __   Activity 10 __ __ __ __

Working Memory – Home Furniture

Intermediate Level

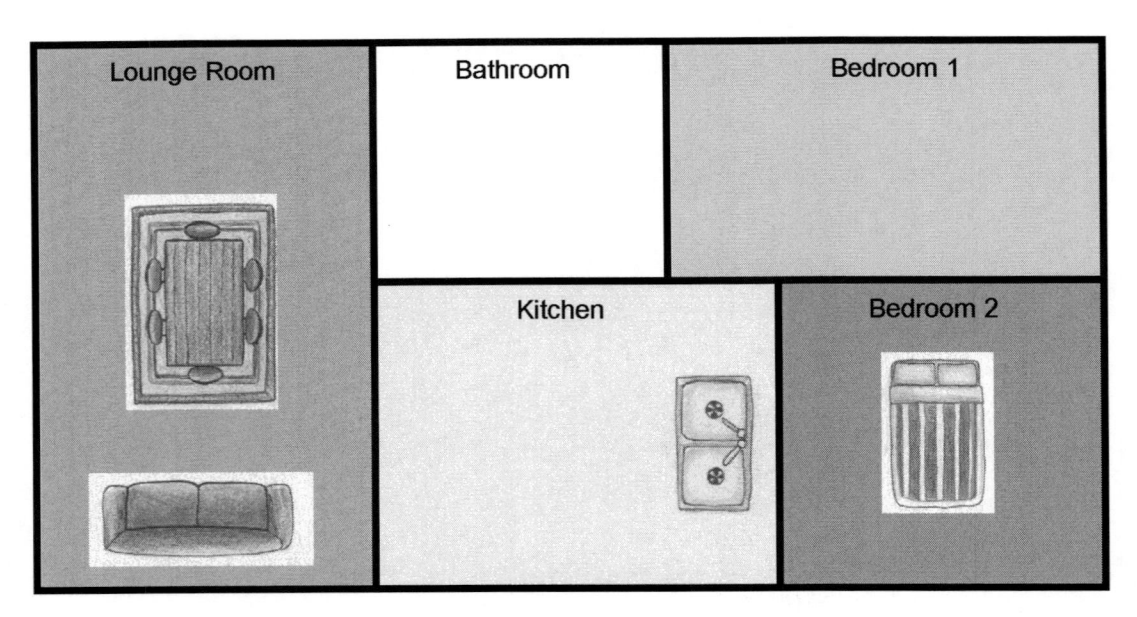

Activity 1

1. Select the dining table, the two seat sofa, the striped bed and the kitchen sink.
2. Place the dining table in the middle of the lounge room and the sofa on the bottom wall of the lounge room.
3. Place the striped bed in the middle of bedroom 2, with the pillows facing the top wall.
4. Place the kitchen sink along the right wall in the kitchen.

Working Memory – Home Furniture

Intermediate Level

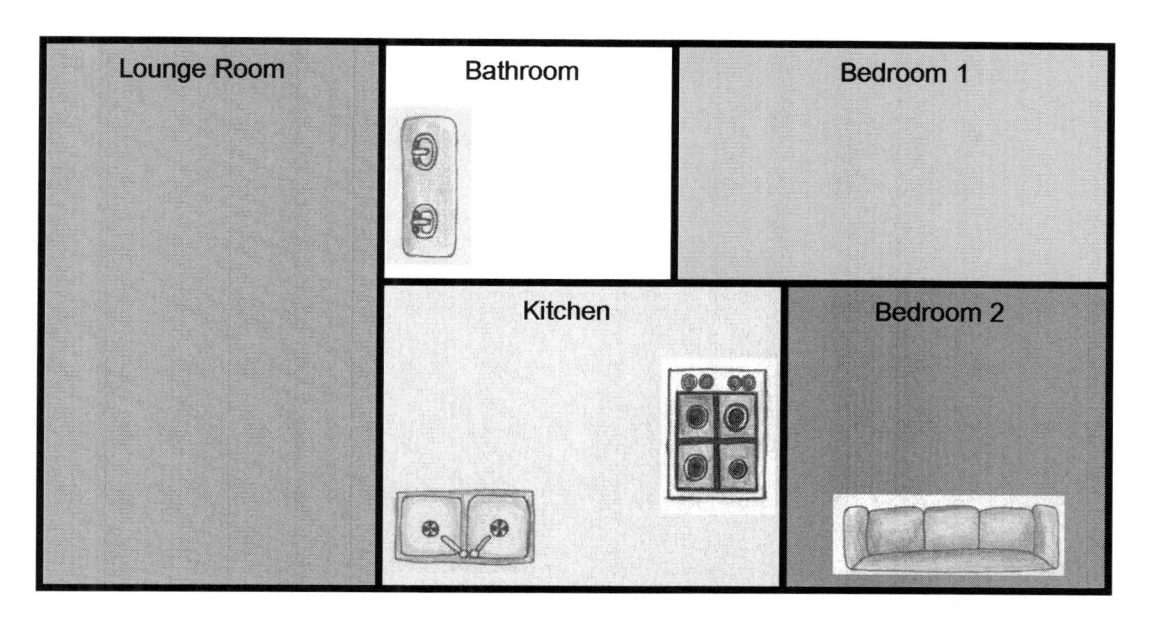

Activity 2

1. Select the bathroom vanity, the three seat sofa, the cooktop and the kitchen sink.
2. Place the kitchen sink in the bottom left corner of the kitchen and the cooktop along the right wall of the kitchen.
3. Place the three seat sofa along the bottom wall of bedroom 2.
4. Place the vanity along the left wall of the bathroom.

Working Memory – Home Furniture

Intermediate Level

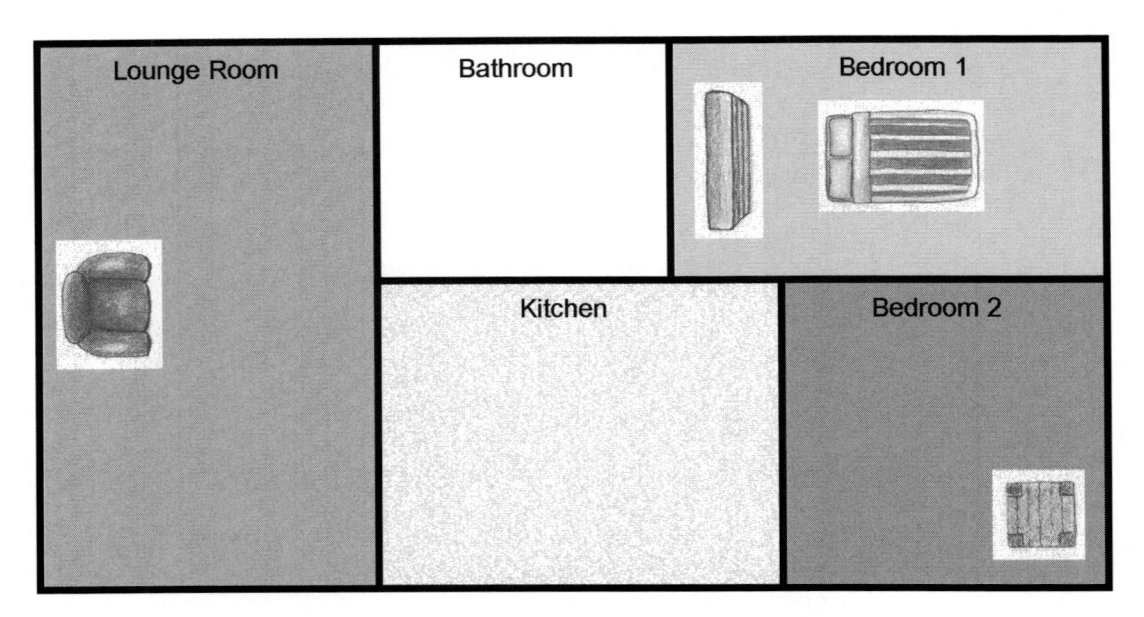

Activity 3

1. Select the side table, the chair, the striped bed and the bookshelf.
2. Place the striped bed in the middle of bedroom 1 and the side table in the bottom right corner of bedroom 2.
3. Place the bookshelf along the left wall of bedroom 1.
4. Place the chair half way up the left wall of the dining room.

Working Memory – Home Furniture

Intermediate Level

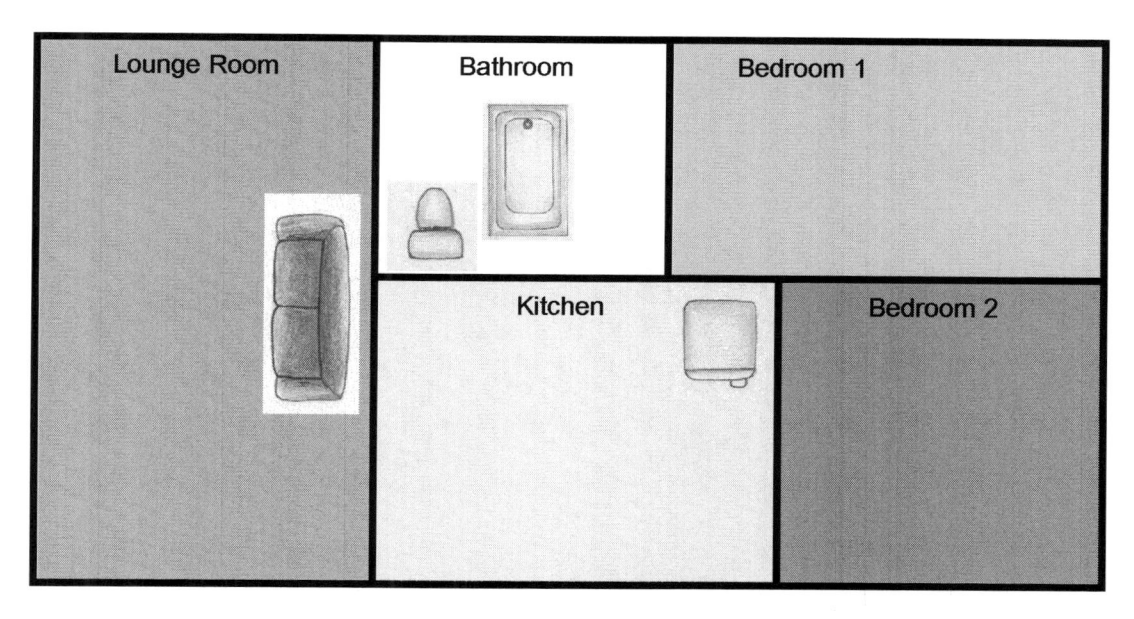

Activity 4

1. Select the two seat sofa, the toilet, the bath and the fridge.
2. Place the toilet in the bottom left corner of the bathroom and the bath in the centre of the bathroom facing up.
3. Place the two seat sofa along the right wall of the dining room half way up.
4. Place the fridge in the top right corner of the kitchen.

Working Memory – Home Furniture

Intermediate Level

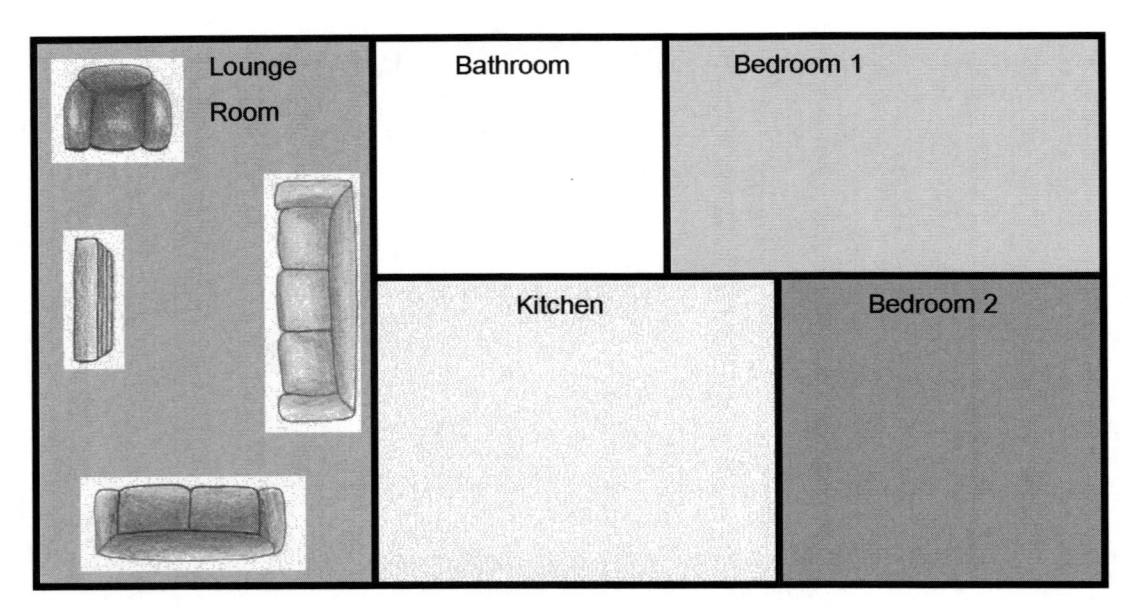

Activity 5

1. Select the two seat sofa, the three seat sofa, the bookshelf and the chair.
2. Place the two seat sofa on the bottom wall of the lounge room and the chair in the top left of the lounge room.
3. Place the three seat sofa half way up the right wall of the lounge room.
4. Place the bookshelf opposite the three seat sofa.

Working Memory – Home Furniture

Intermediate Level

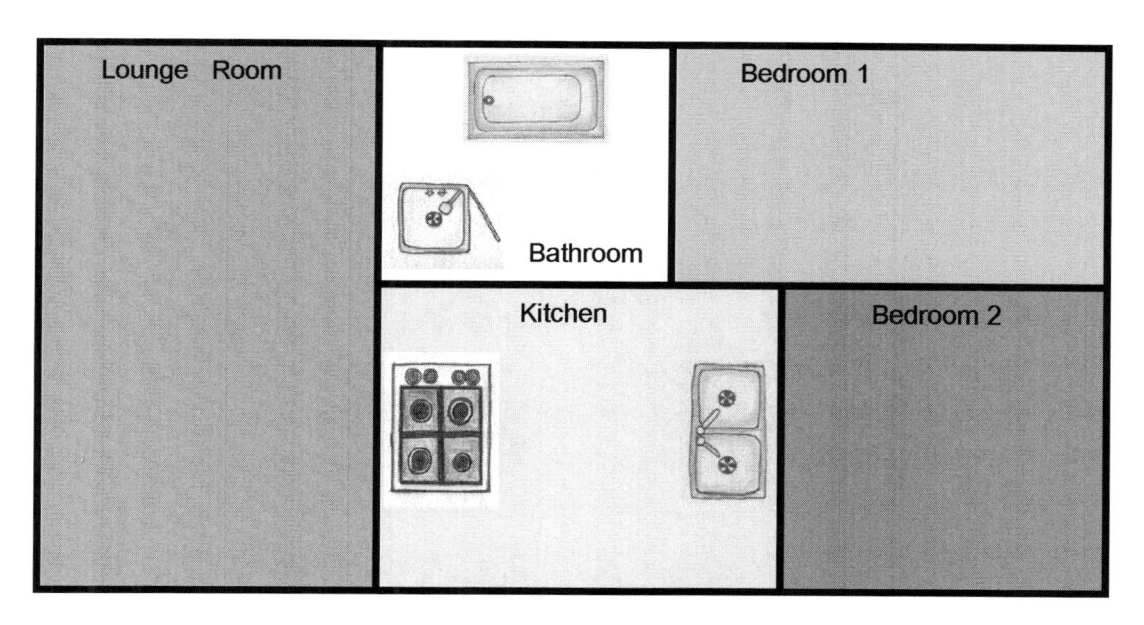

Activity 6

1. Select the bath, the shower, the kitchen sink and the cooktop.
2. Place the cooktop along the left wall of the kitchen and the kitchen sink along the right wall of the kitchen.
3. Place the bath along the top of the bathroom in the middle.
4. Place the shower in the bottom left corner of the bathroom.

Working Memory – Home Furniture

Intermediate Level

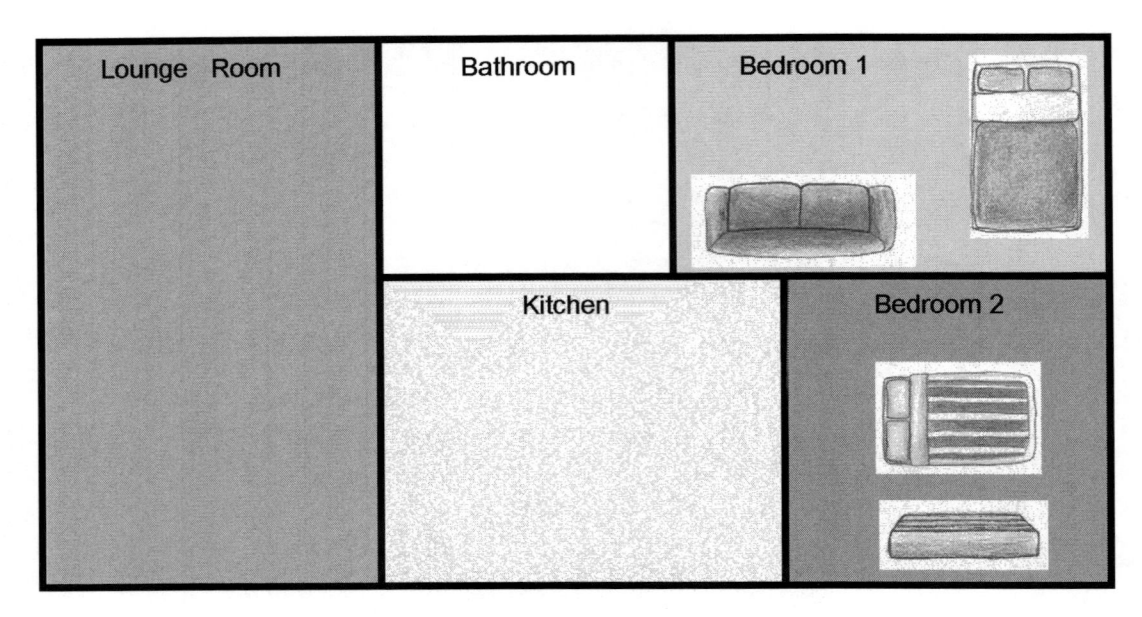

Activity 7

1. Select the plain bed, the striped bed, the two seat sofa and the bookshelf.
2. Place the plain bed along the right wall of bedroom 1 facing up and the striped bed in the middle of bedroom 2.
3. Place the bookshelf along the bottom wall of bedroom 2.
4. Place the two seat sofa in the bottom left corner of bedroom 1.

Working Memory – Home Furniture

Intermediate Level

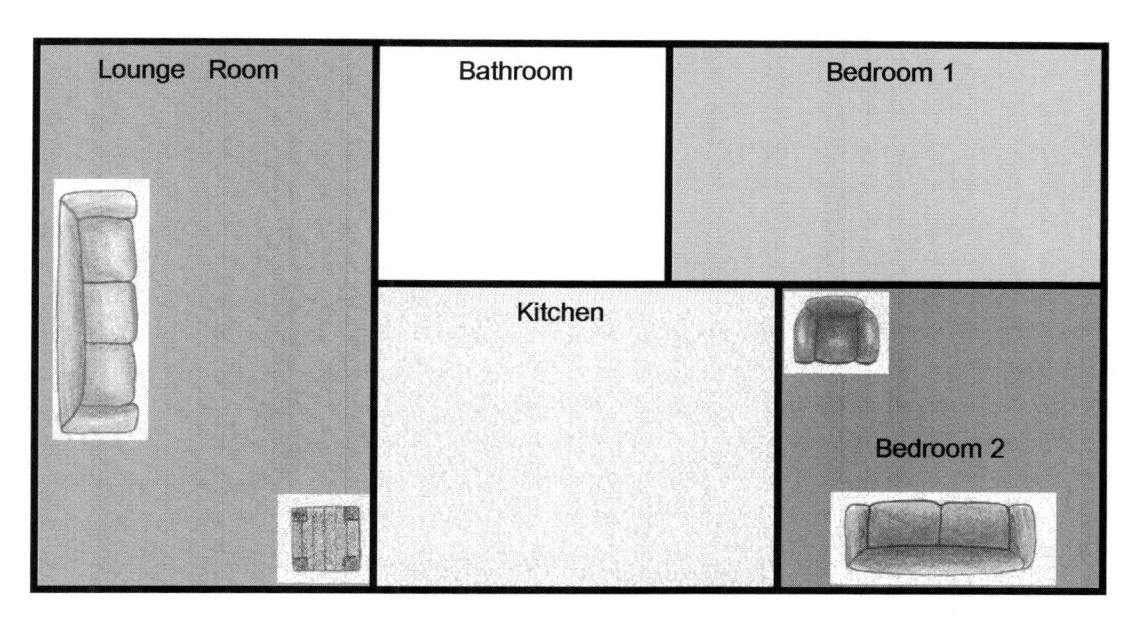

Activity 8

1. Select the three seat sofa, the side table, the chair and the two seat sofa.
2. Place the three seat sofa half way up the left wall of the lounge room and the chair in the top left corner of bedroom 2.
3. Place the two seat sofa on the bottom wall of bedroom 2.
4. Place the side table in the bottom right corner of the lounge room.

Working Memory – Home Furniture

Intermediate Level

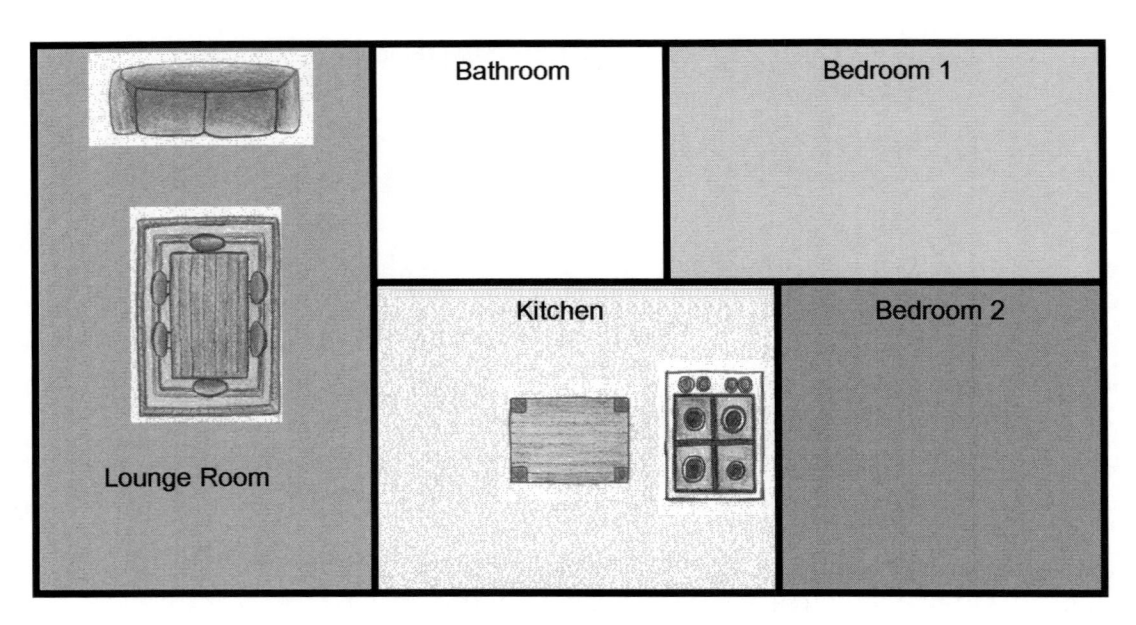

Activity 9

1. Select the dining table, the kitchen table, the cooktop and the two seat sofa.
2. Place the dining table in the centre of the lounge room and the kitchen table in the centre of the kitchen.
3. Place the two seat sofa along the top wall in the lounge room.
4. Place the cooktop along the right wall of the kitchen.

Working Memory – Home Furniture

Intermediate Level

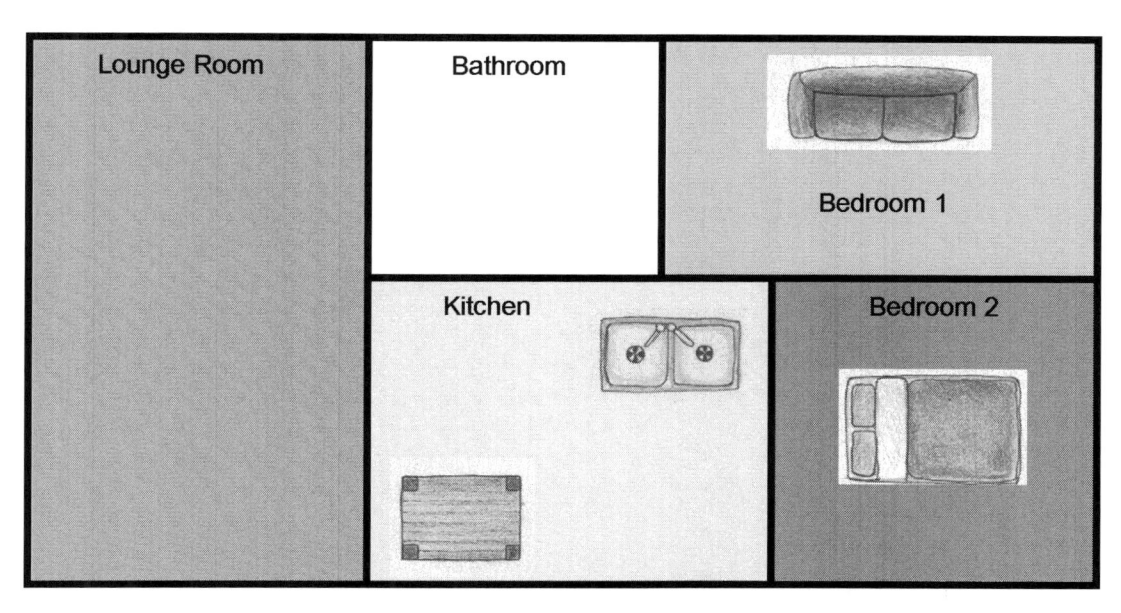

Activity 10

1. Select the kitchen table, the kitchen sink, the two seat sofa and the plain bed.
2. Place the kitchen table in the bottom left corner of the kitchen and the kitchen sink in the top right corner of the kitchen.
3. Place the plain bed in the middle of bedroom 2.
4. Place the two seat sofa along the top wall of bedroom 1 in the middle.

Working Memory - Furniture

Record Sheet

Tick √ for correct and ✗ for incorrect

Intermediate Level

1. Activity __ __ __ __   6. Activity __ __ __ __

2. Activty   __ __ __ __   7. Activity __ __ __ __

3. Activity __ __ __ __   8. Activity __ __ __ __

4. Activity __ __ __ __   9. Activity __ __ __ __

5. Activity __ __ __ __   10. Activity __ __ __ __

Working Memory – Home Furniture

Advanced Level

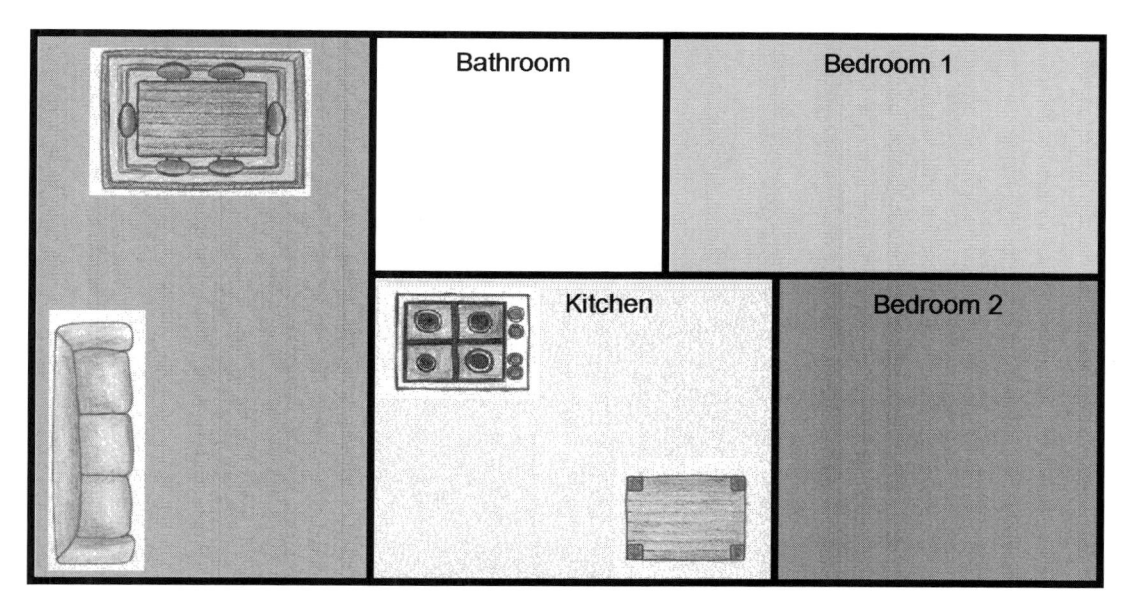

Activity 1

1. Select the dining table, the kitchen table, the cooktop and the three seat sofa.
2. Place the kitchen table in the bottom right corner of the kitchen and the cooktop in the top left corner of the kitchen.
3. Stand the three seat sofa in the bottom left corner of the lounge room.
4. Place the dining table along the top wall of the lounge room in the middle.

Working Memory – Home Furniture

Advanced Level

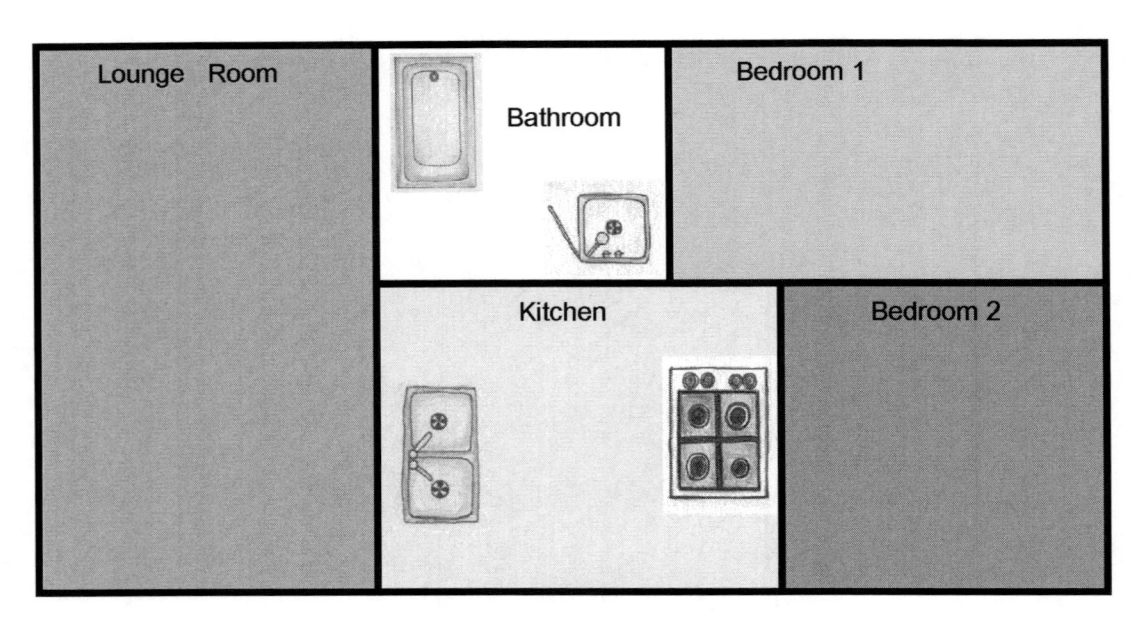

Activity 2

1. Select the bath, the shower, the kitchen sink and the cooktop.
2. Before placing the sink along the left wall of the kitchen, place the cooktop along the right wall of the kitchen.
3. Place the bath in the top left corner of the bathroom facing up.
4. Place the shower in the bottom right corner of the bathroom.

Working Memory – Home Furniture

Advanced Level

Activity 3

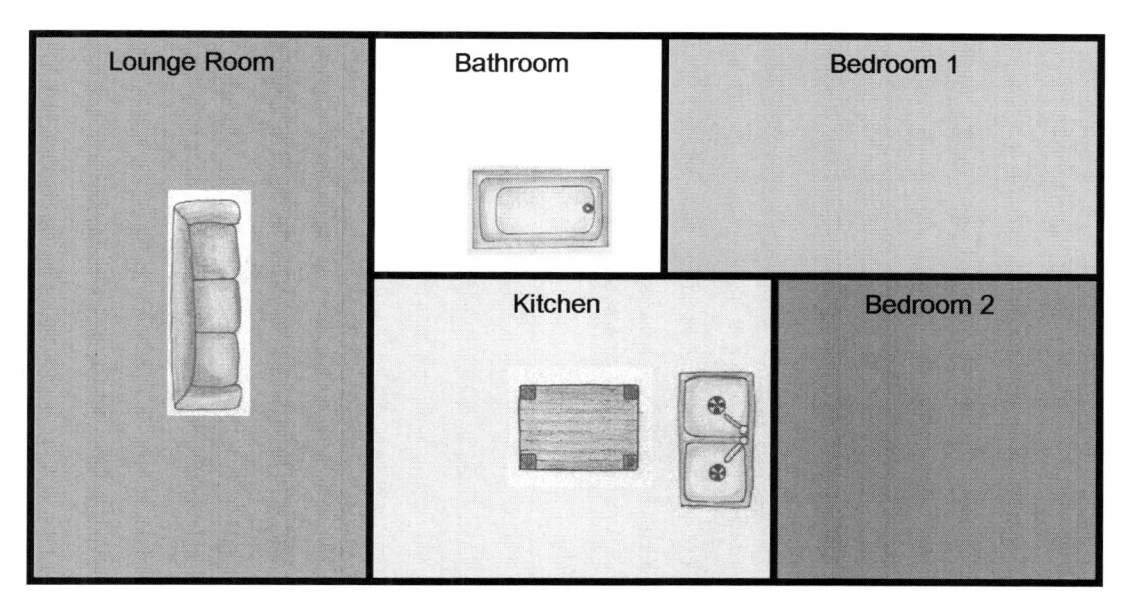

1. Select the bath, the three seat sofa, the kitchen table and the kitchen sink.
2. Before you place the kitchen table in the middle of the kitchen, place the three seat sofa in the middle of the lounge room.
3. Place the kitchen sink along the right wall of the kitchen.
4. Place the bath along the bottom wall of the bathroom in the middle.

Working Memory – Home Furniture

Advanced Level

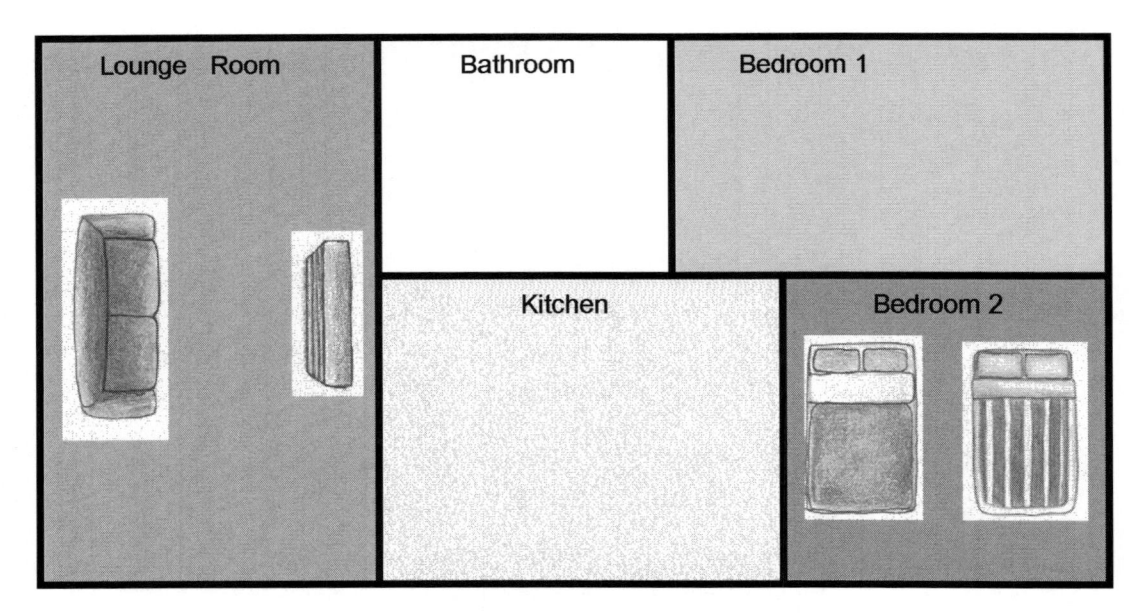

Activity 4

1. Select the plain bed, the striped bed, the two seat sofa and the bookshelf.

2. After placing the plain bed along the left wall of bedroom 2, place the striped bed beside it in bedroom 2.

3. Place the bookshelf along the right wall of the lounge room in the middle.

4. Place the two seat sofa opposite the bookshelf in the lounge room

Working Memory – Home Furniture

Advanced Level

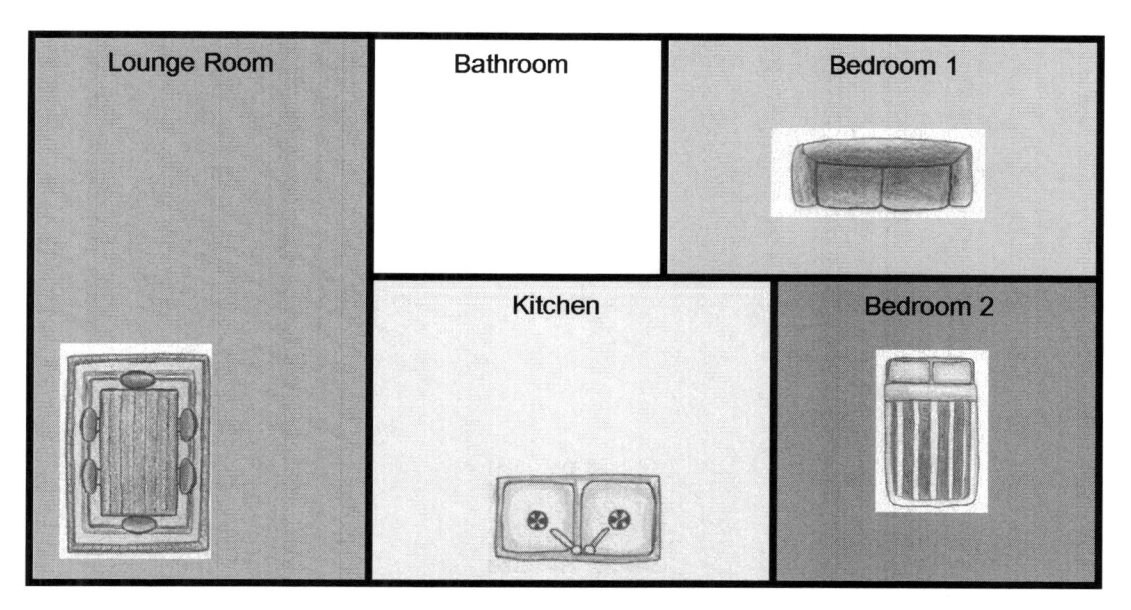

Activity 5

1. Select the dining table, the two seat sofa, the striped bed and the kitchen sink.
2. Place the dining table in the bottom left corner of the lounge room and the sink along the bottom wall of the kitchen in the middle.
3. Place the striped bed in the middle of bedroom 2 facing up.
4. Place the two seat sofa in the middle of bedroom 1.

Working Memory – Home Furniture

Advanced Level

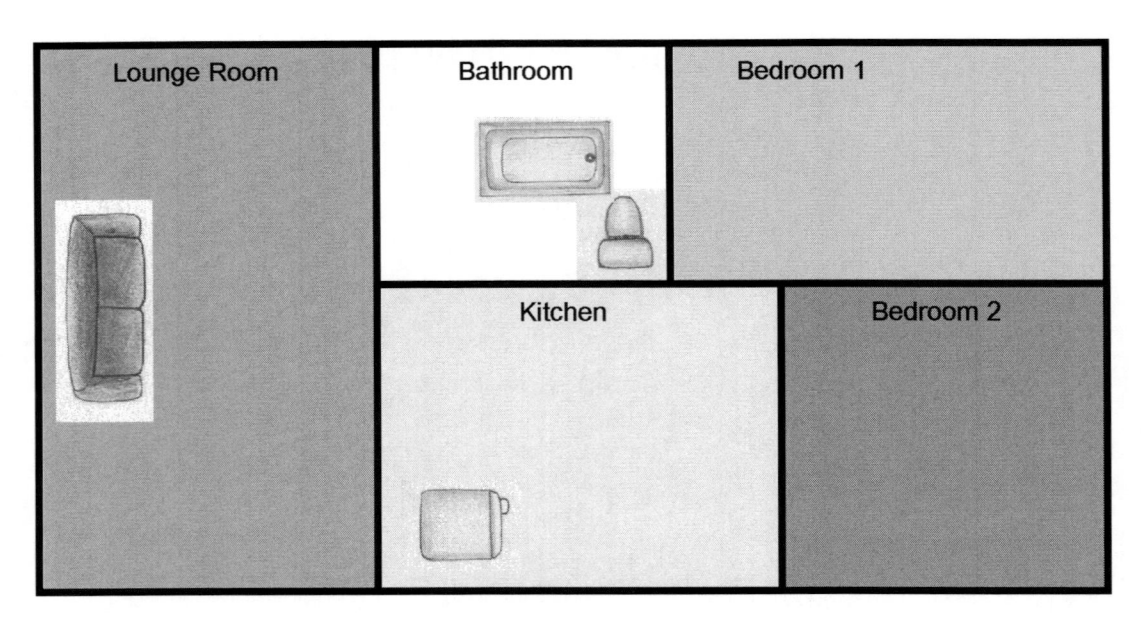

Activity 6

1. Select the two seat sofa, the toilet, the bath and the fridge.
2. Before placing the toilet in the bottom right corner of the bathroom, place the bath in the centre of the bathroom.
3. Place the two seat sofa along the left wall of the lounge room half way up.
4. Place the fridge in the bottom left corner of the kitchen.

Working Memory – Home Furniture

Advanced Level

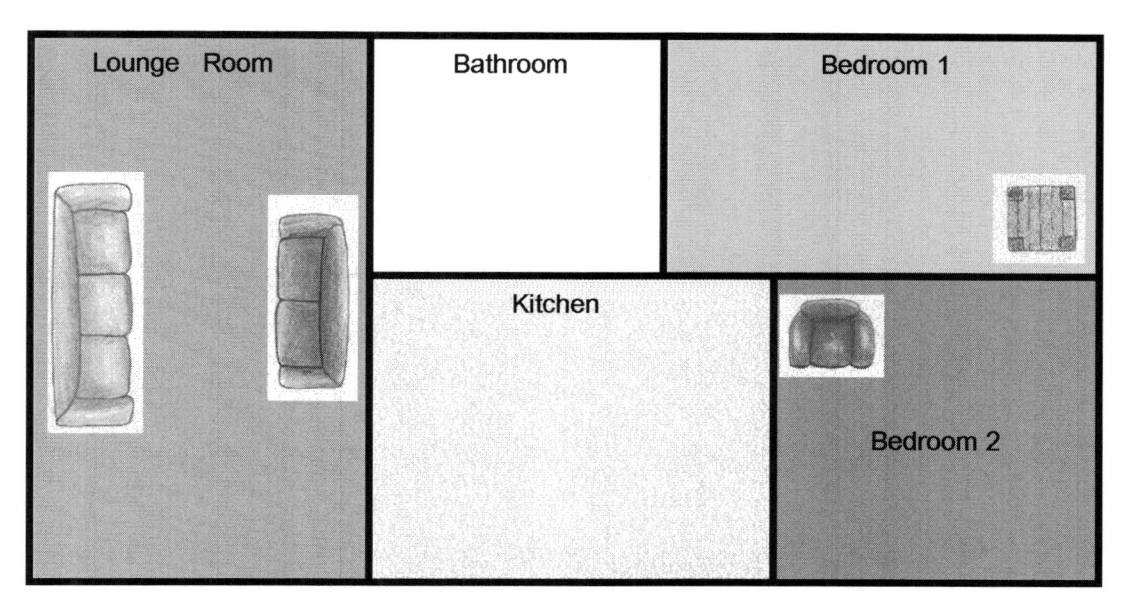

Activity 7

1. Select the three seat sofa, the side table, the chair and the two seat sofa.
2. After placing the side table in the bottom right corner of bedroom 1, place the chair in the top left corner of bedroom 2.
3. Place the two seat sofa half way up the right wall of the lounge room.
4. Place the three seat sofa opposite the two seat sofa.

Working Memory – Home Furniture

Advanced Level

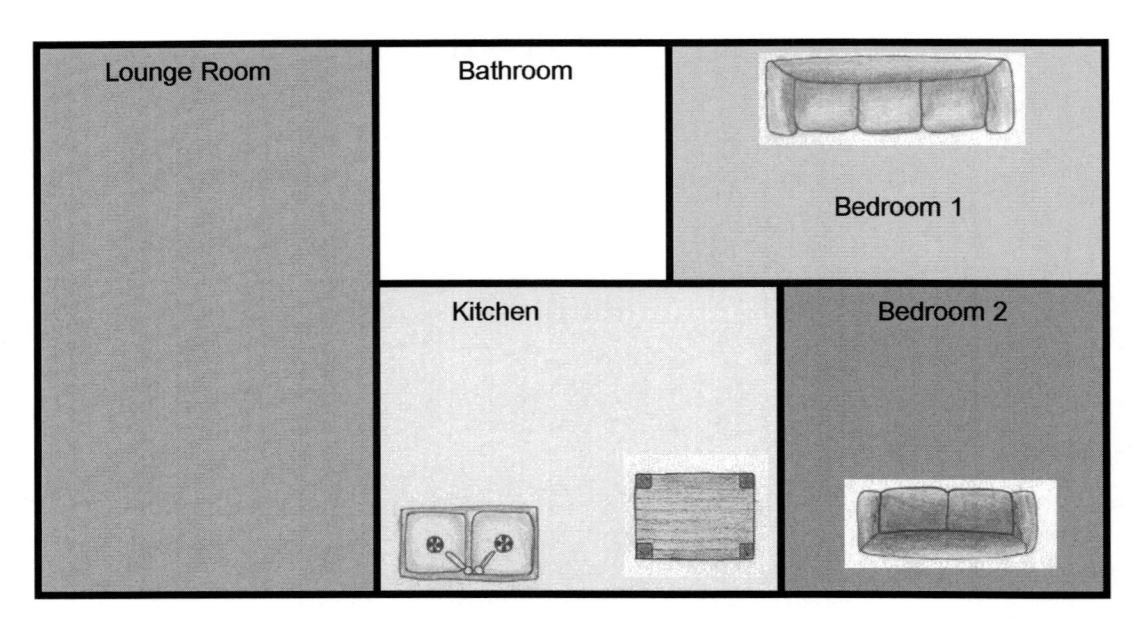

Activity 8

1. Select the kitchen table, the kitchen sink, the two seat sofa and the three seat sofa.
2. Before you place the kitchen table in the bottom right corner of the kitchen, place the kitchen sink in the bottom left corner of the kitchen.
3. Place the two seat sofa on the bottom wall of bedroom 2.
4. Place the three seat sofa on the top wall of bedroom 1.

Working Memory – Home Furniture

Advanced Level

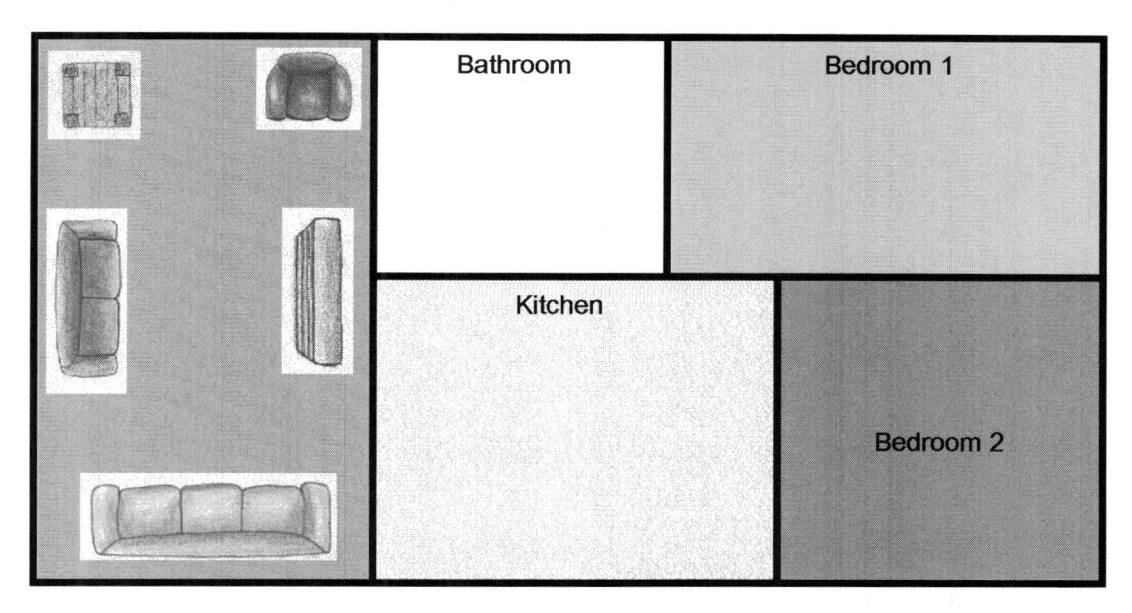

Activity 9

1. Select the three seat sofa, the side table, the chair, the two seat sofa and the bookshelf.

2. After placing the side table in the top left corner of the lounge room, place the chair in the top right corner of the lounge room.

3. Place the two seat sofa half way up the left wall of the lounge room and the bookshelf opposite it.

4. Place the three seat sofa along the bottom wall of the lounge room.

Working Memory – Home Furniture

Advanced Level

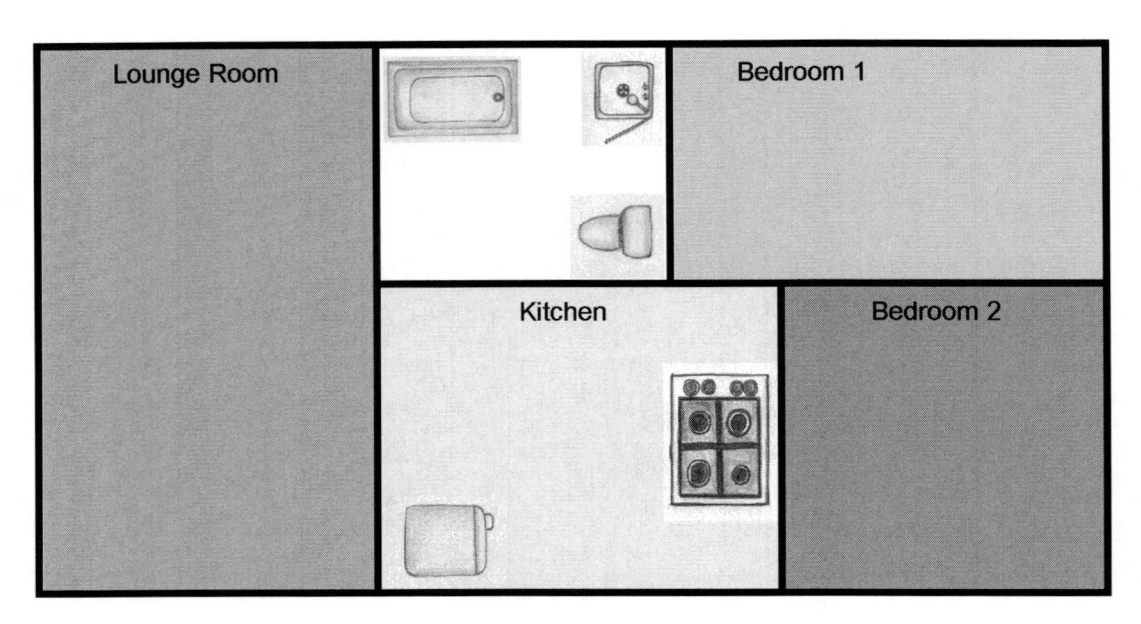

Activity 10

1. Select the toilet, the bath, the shower, the fridge and the cooktop.

2. Before placing the toilet in the bottom right corner of the bathroom, place the bath in the top left corner.

3. After placing the fridge in the bottom left corner of the kitchen, place the cooktop along the right wall of the kitchen, halfway up.

4. Place the shower in the top right corner of the bathroom.

Working Memory - Furniture

Record Sheet

Tick √ for correct and ✗ for incorrect

Advanced Level

1. Activity __ __ __ __
2. Activty __ __ __ __
3. Activity __ __ __ __
4. Activity __ __ __ __
5. Activity __ __ __ __

6. Activity __ __ __ __
7. Activity __ __ __ __
8. Activity __ __ __ __
9. Activity __ __ __ __
10. Activity __ __ __ __

Section 6

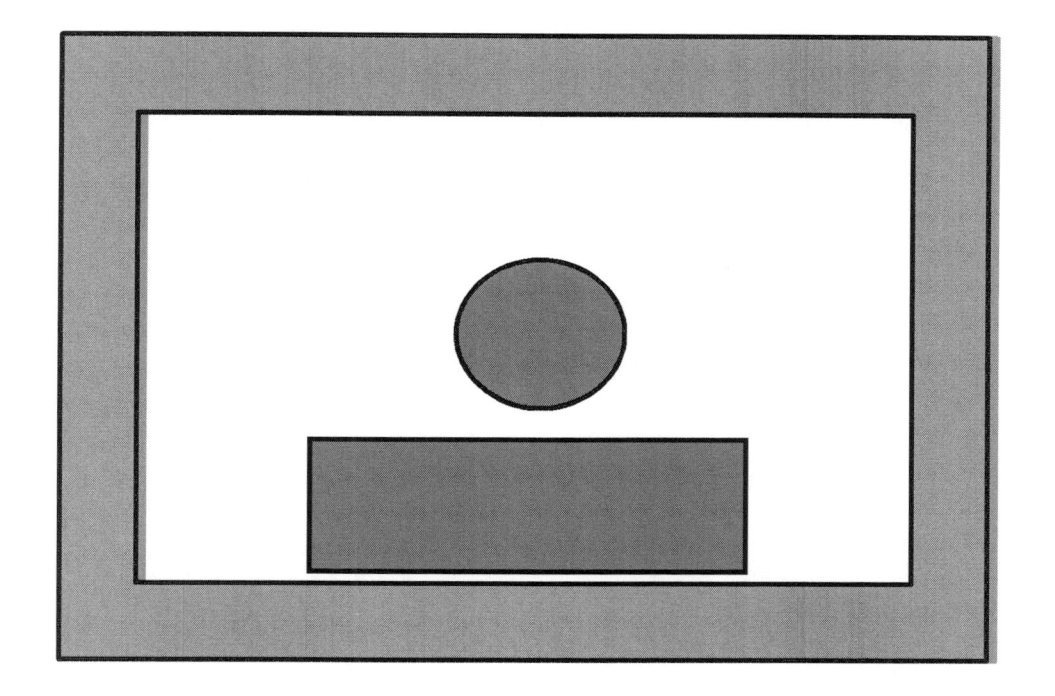

Working Memory Boxes

Important: Please note that for **all responses** students may not begin the activity until the clinician has <u>completed</u> the directions.

Working Memory Boxes

Instructions

The activities in this section prompt children to move shapes within the confines of a box to a pre-set range of oral questions. This section is *entry* level.

You will need...

- A photocopied sheet of the individual shapes
- A photocopied sheet of the shapes box
- A pair of scissors
- A laminator (optional)

Cut out and laminate the shapes. Present all the shapes and the box to the child. Read the **directions** to the child in a clear voice and at a slow rate. Make certain the child cannot see the correct answers while they are placing the shapes within the box. Some children, depending on their abilities, may require the questions to be repeated. After each activity, show the child how their efforts matched with the example boxes. If a child has some difficulty with the *entry* level activities, redo the *entry* level and provide extra scaffolding for the child as needed before venturing on to the *Intermediate* level.

Working Memory Shapes

Cut out each shape and laminate for increased durability. It's also helpful to attach a small square piece of card below each laminated shape to provide a separation from the page. This makes the shapes far easier to grasp and move.

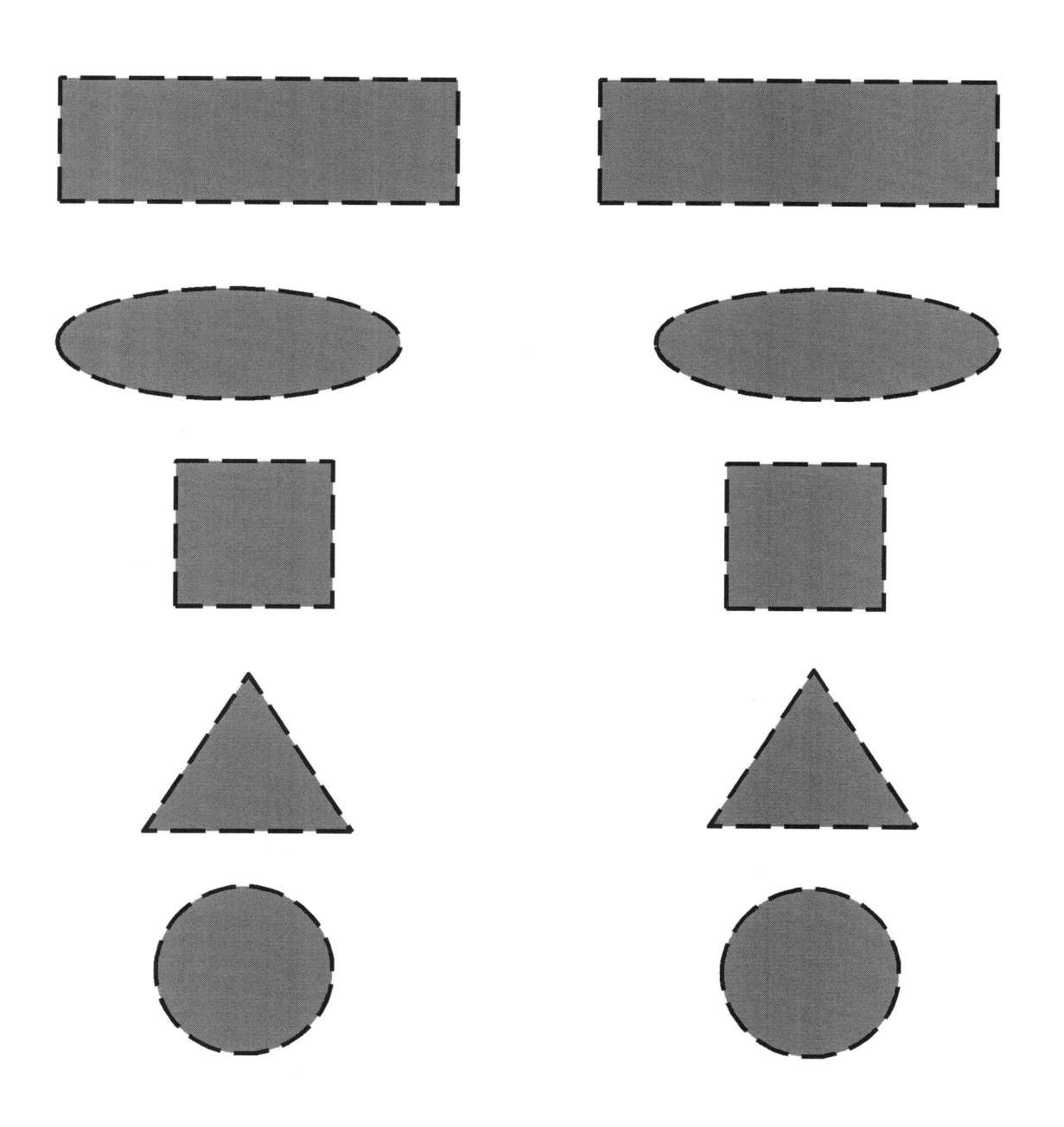

Working Memory Shapes Box

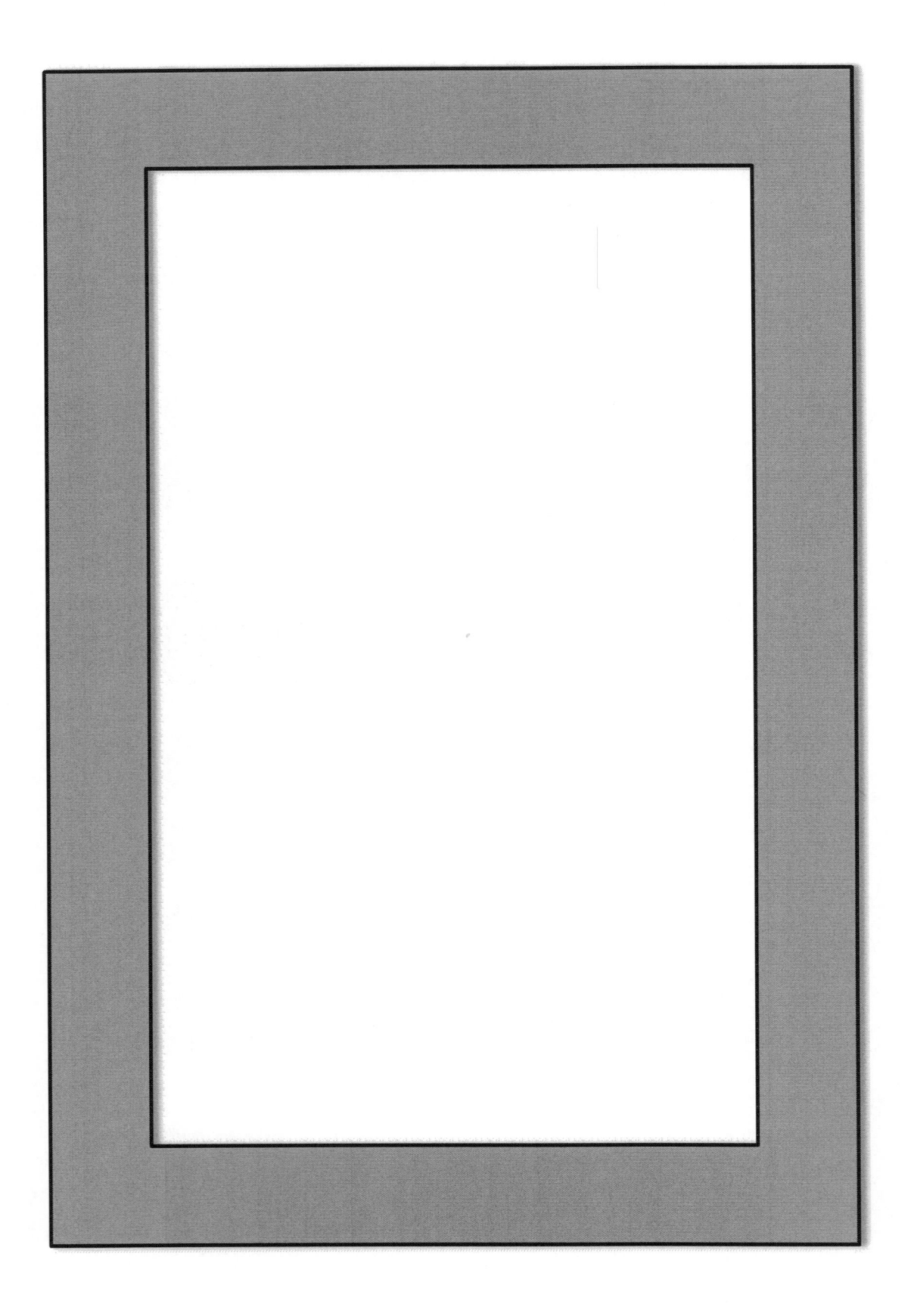

Working Memory Boxes

Entry Level

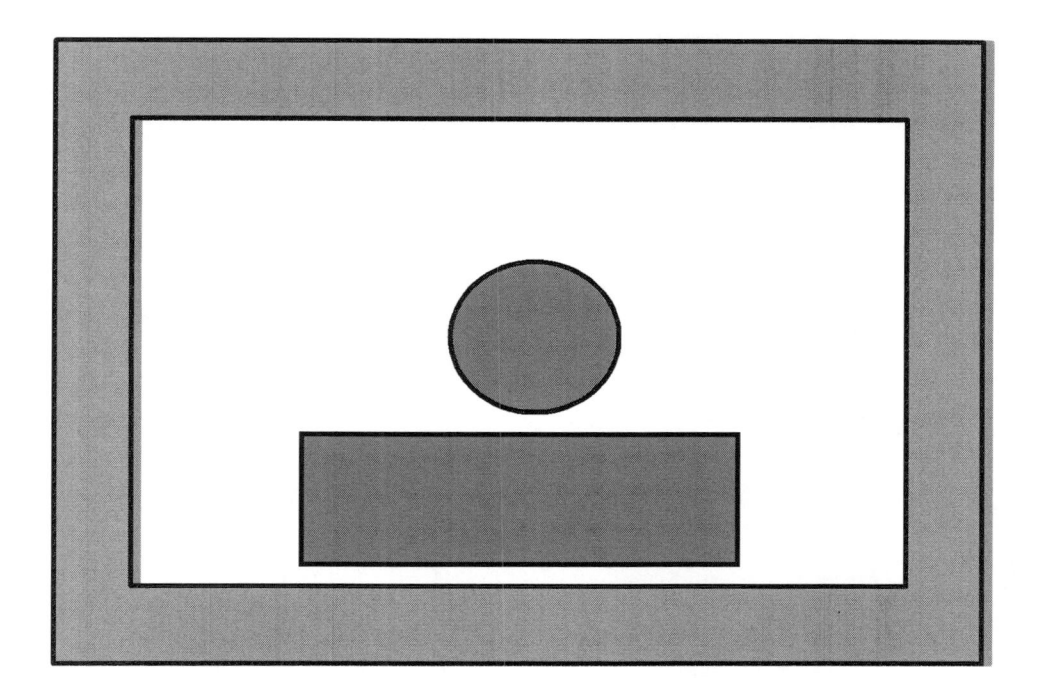

Activity 1

1. Select a rectangle and a circle.
2. Place the rectangle on its side in the middle of the box on the bottom.
3. Place the circle in the middle of the box above the rectangle.

Working Memory Boxes

Entry Level

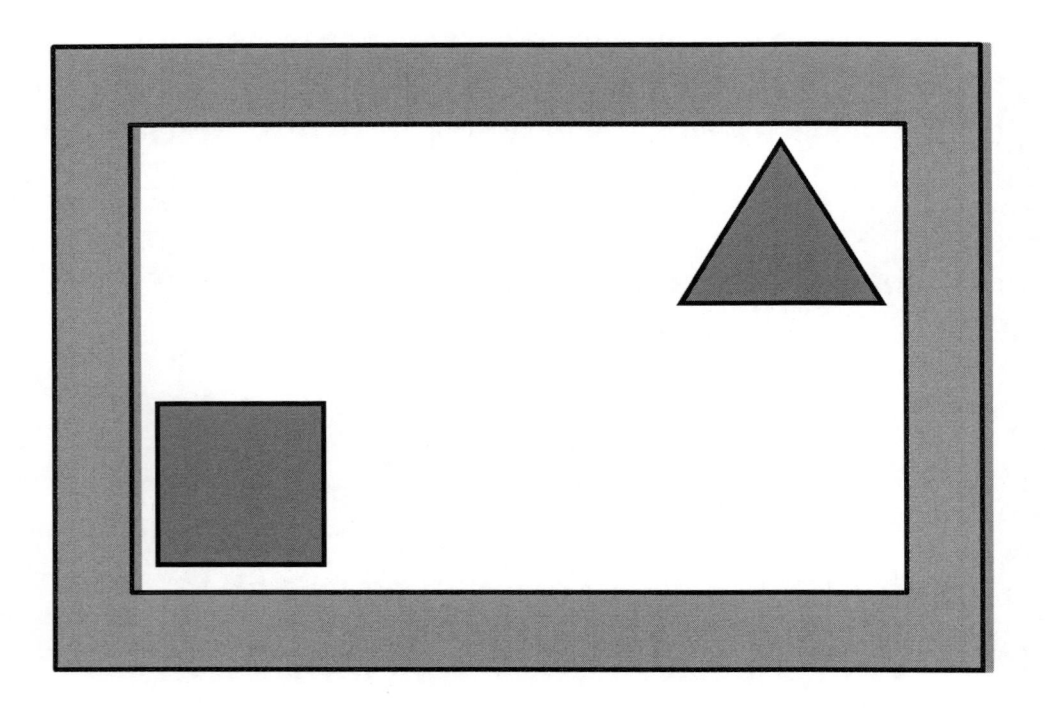

Activity 2

1. Select a square and a triangle.

2. Place the square in the bottom left corner of the box.

3. Place the triangle in the top right corner of the box.

Working Memory Boxes

Entry Level

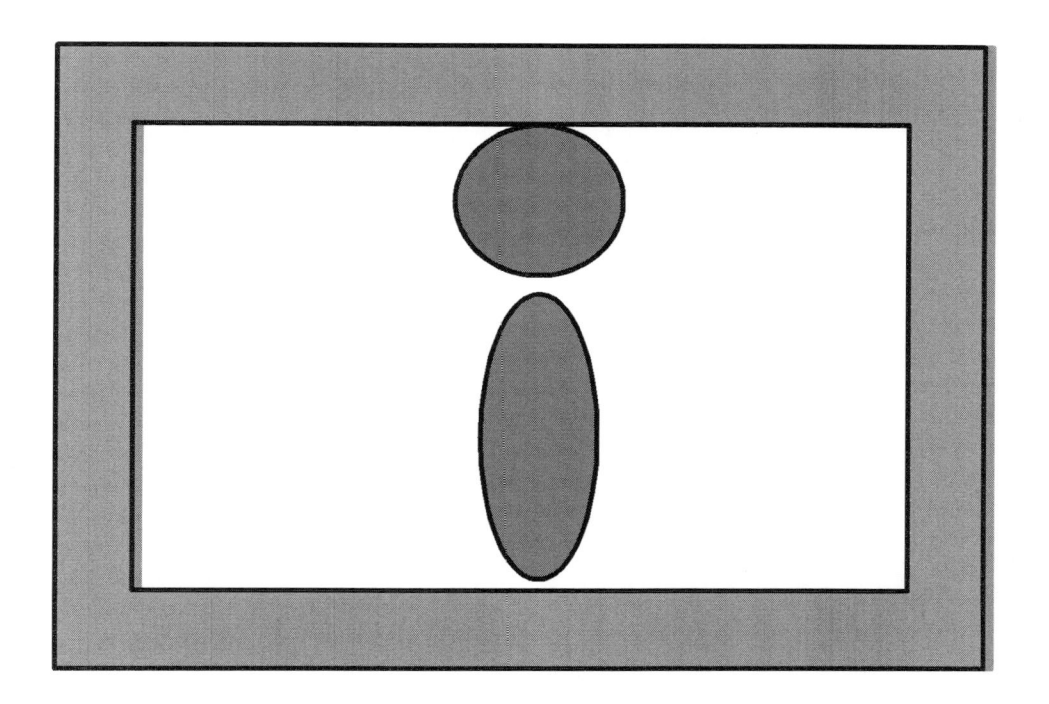

Activity 3

1. Select an oval and a circle.
2. Stand the oval on its end on the bottom of the box in the middle.
3. Place the circle on top of the oval.

Working Memory Boxes

Entry Level

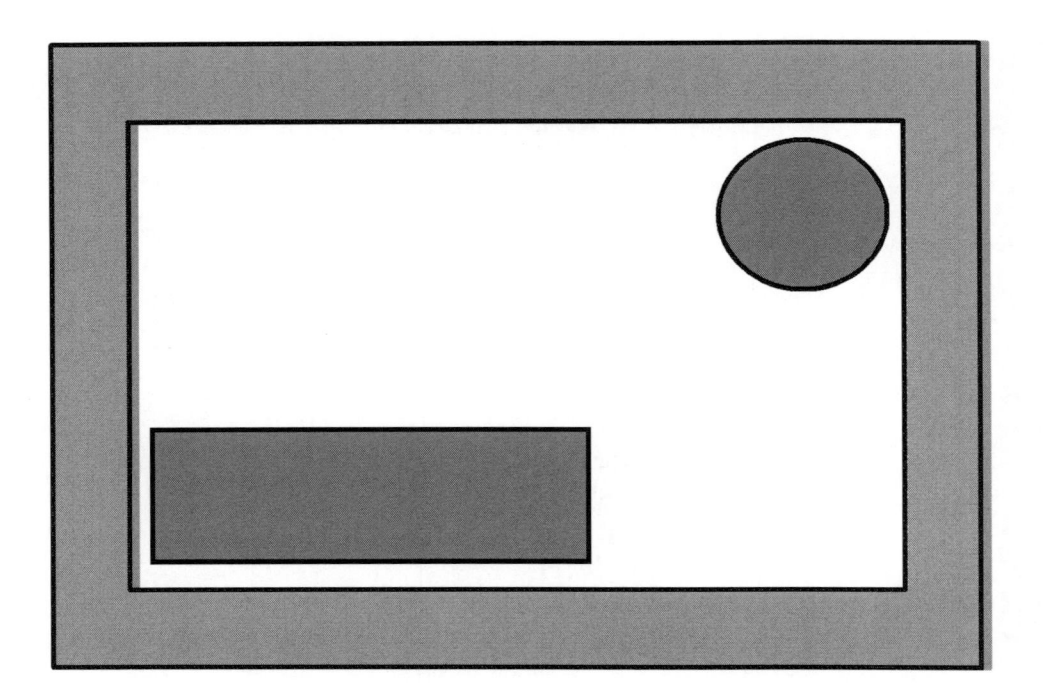

Activity 4

1. Select a rectangle and a circle.
2. Place the rectangle on its side in the bottom left corner of the box.
3. Place the circle in the top right corner of the box.

Working Memory Boxes

Entry Level

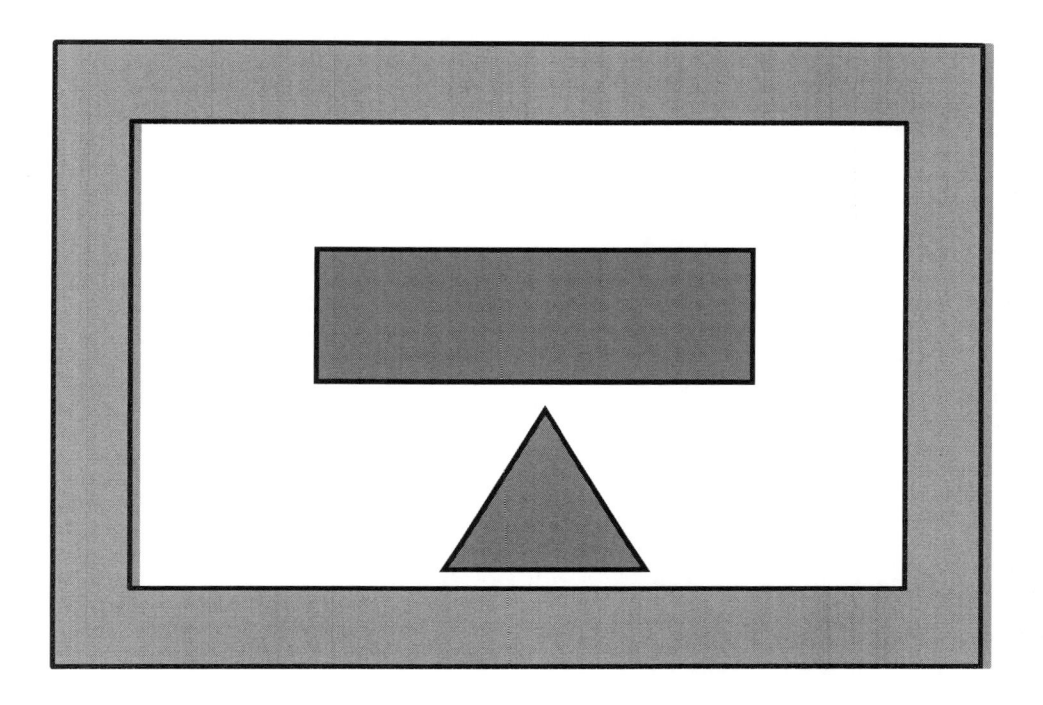

Activity 5

1. Select a rectangle and a triangle.

2. Place the rectangle on its side in the middle of the box.

3. Place the triangle in the middle of the box on the bottom.

Working Memory Boxes

Entry Level

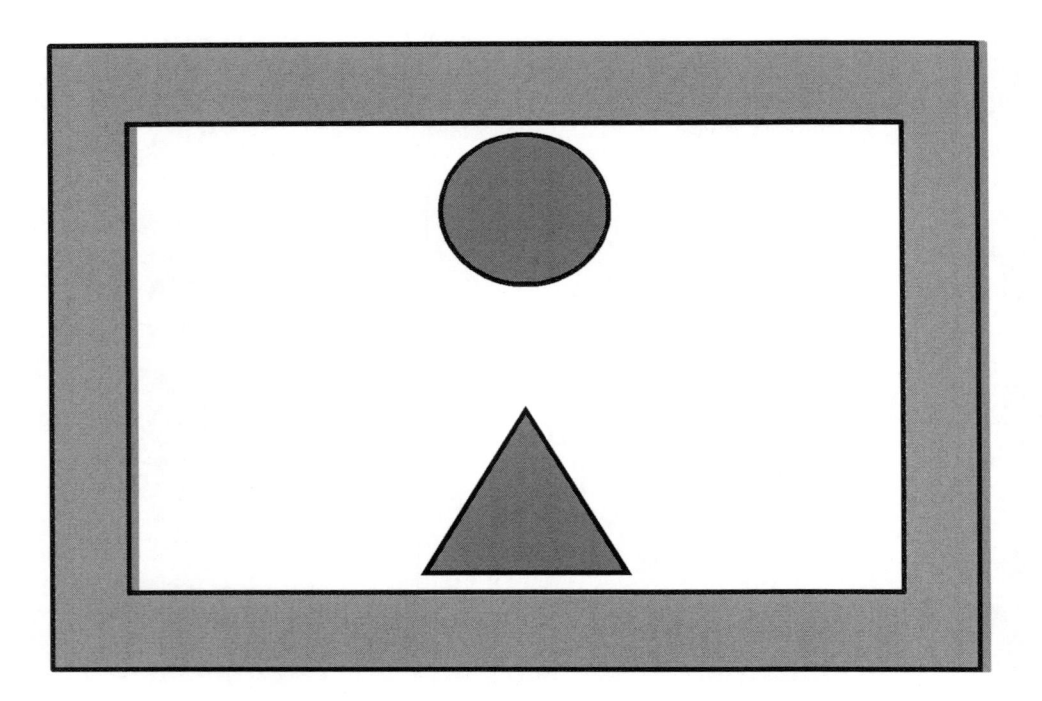

Activity 6

1. Select a circle and a triangle.

2. Place the circle at the top of the box in the middle.

3. Place the triangle in the middle of the box on the bottom.

Working Memory Boxes

Entry Level

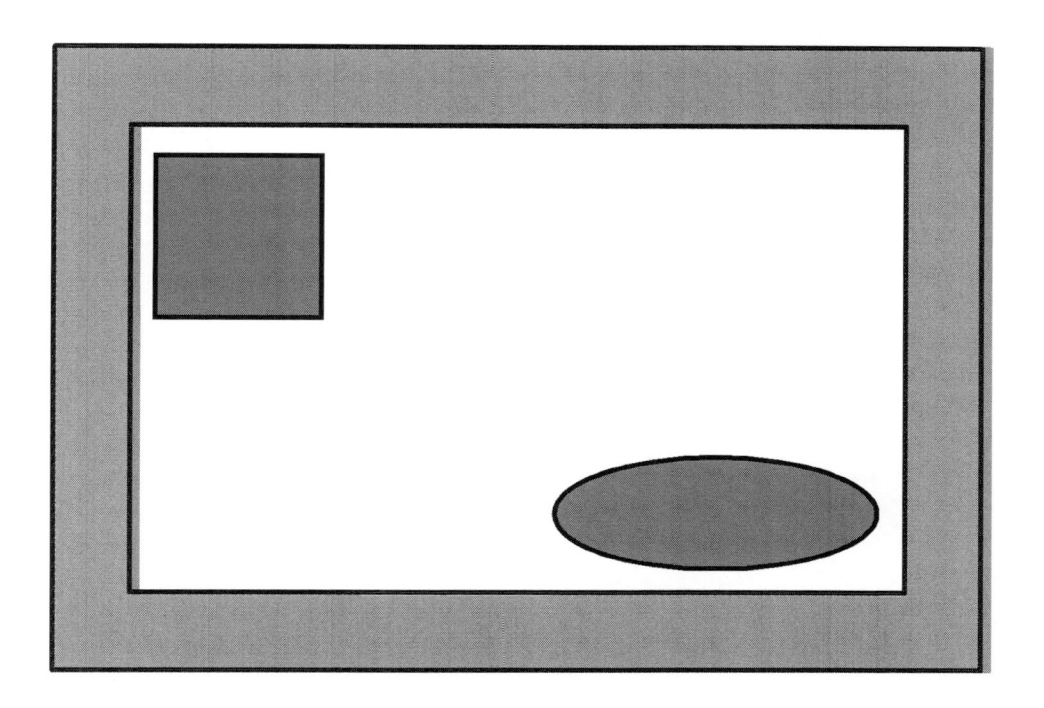

Activity 7

1. Select a square and an oval.
2. Place the square in the top left corner of the box.
3. Place the oval in the bottom right corner of the box.

Working Memory Boxes

Entry Level

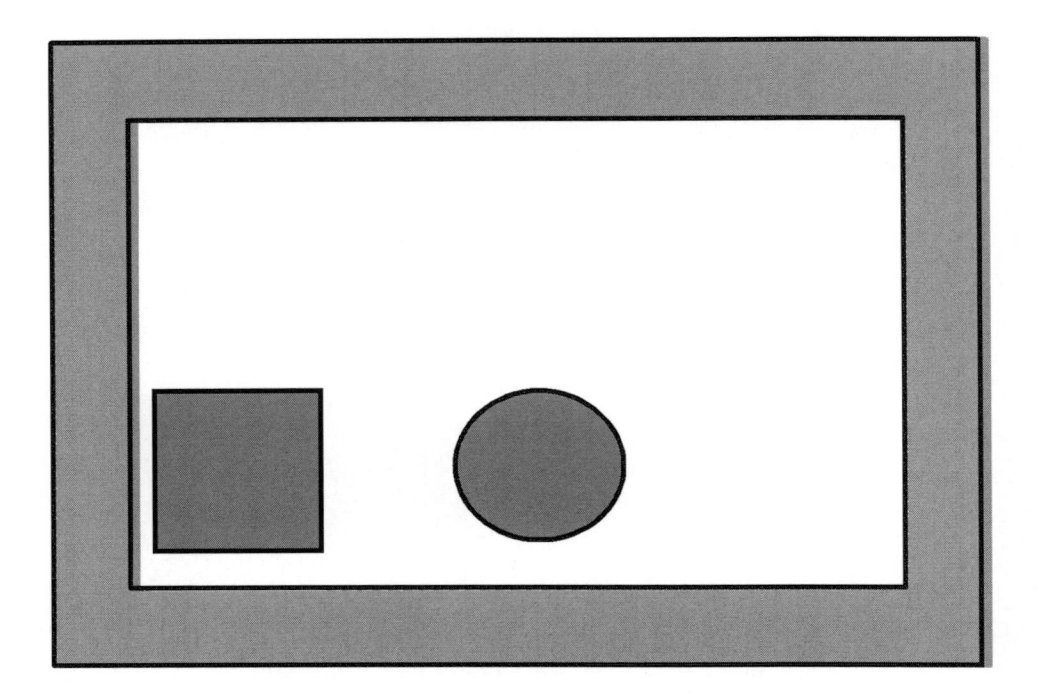

Activity 8

1. Select a square and a circle.

2. Place the square in the bottom left corner of the box.

3. Place the circle in the middle of the box on the bottom.

Working Memory Boxes

Entry Level

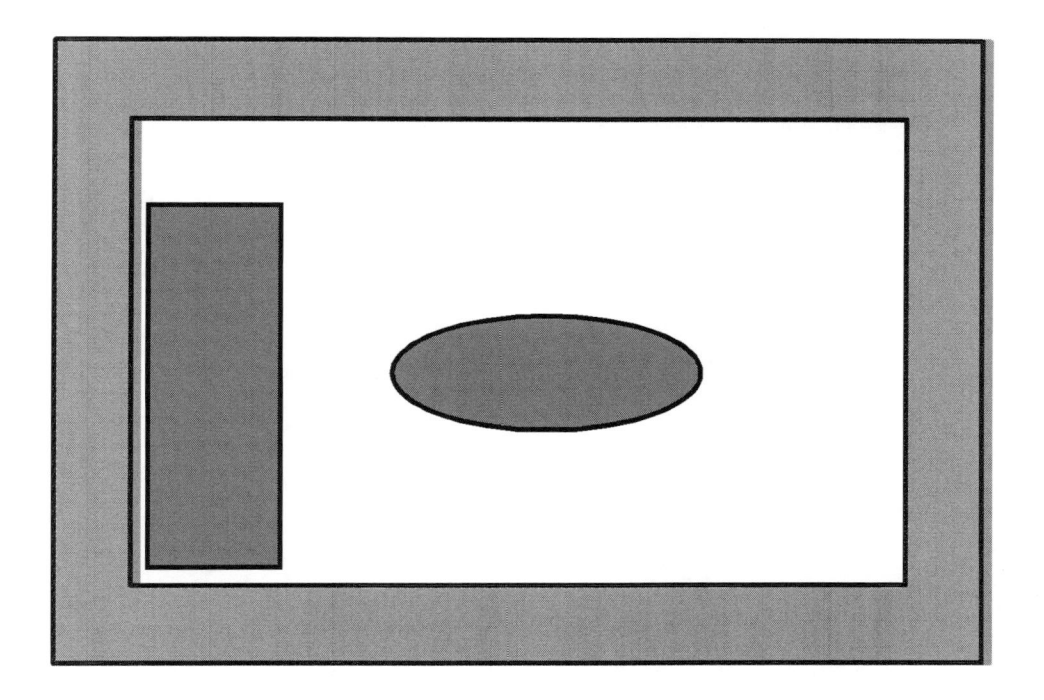

Activity 9

1. Select a rectangle and an oval.
2. Stand the rectangle on its end in the bottom left corner of the box.
3. Place the rectangle on its side in the middle of the box.

Working Memory Boxes

Entry Level

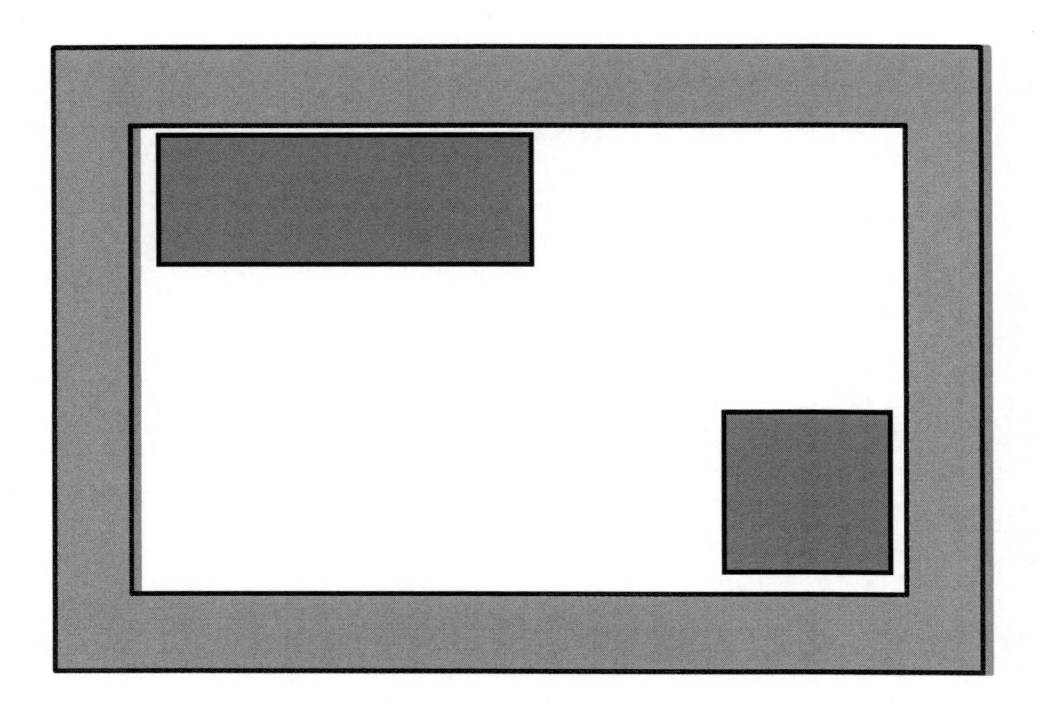

Activity 10

1. Select a rectangle and a square.

2. Place the rectangle on its side in the top left corner of the box.

3. Place the square in the bottom right corner of the box.

Working Memory Boxes

Record Sheet

Tick √ for correct and ✗ for incorrect

Entry Level

1. Activity __ __ __

2. Activty __ __ __

3. Activity __ __ __

4. Activity __ __ __

5. Activity __ __ __

6. Activity __ __ __

7. Activity __ __ __

8. Activity __ __ __

9. Activity __ __ __

10. Activity __ __ __

Working Memory Boxes

Intermediate Level

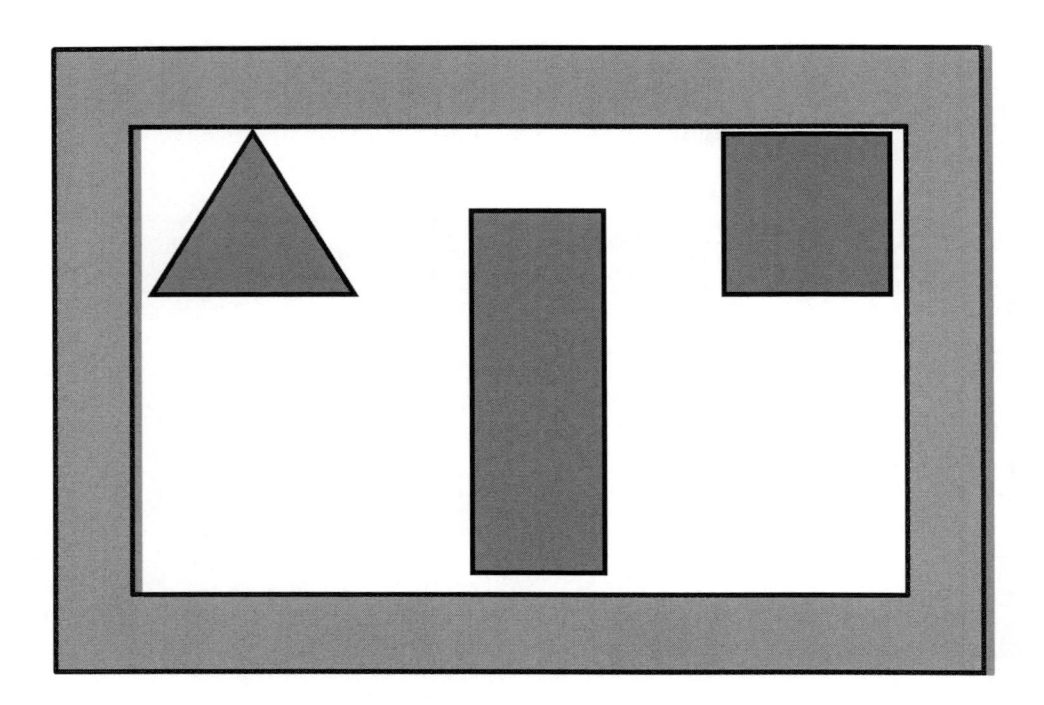

Activity 1

1. Select a rectangle, a square and a triangle.
2. Stand the rectangle on its end in the middle of the box on the bottom.
3. Place the square in the top right corner of the box.
4. Place the triangle in the top left corner of the box.

Working Memory Boxes

Intermediate Level

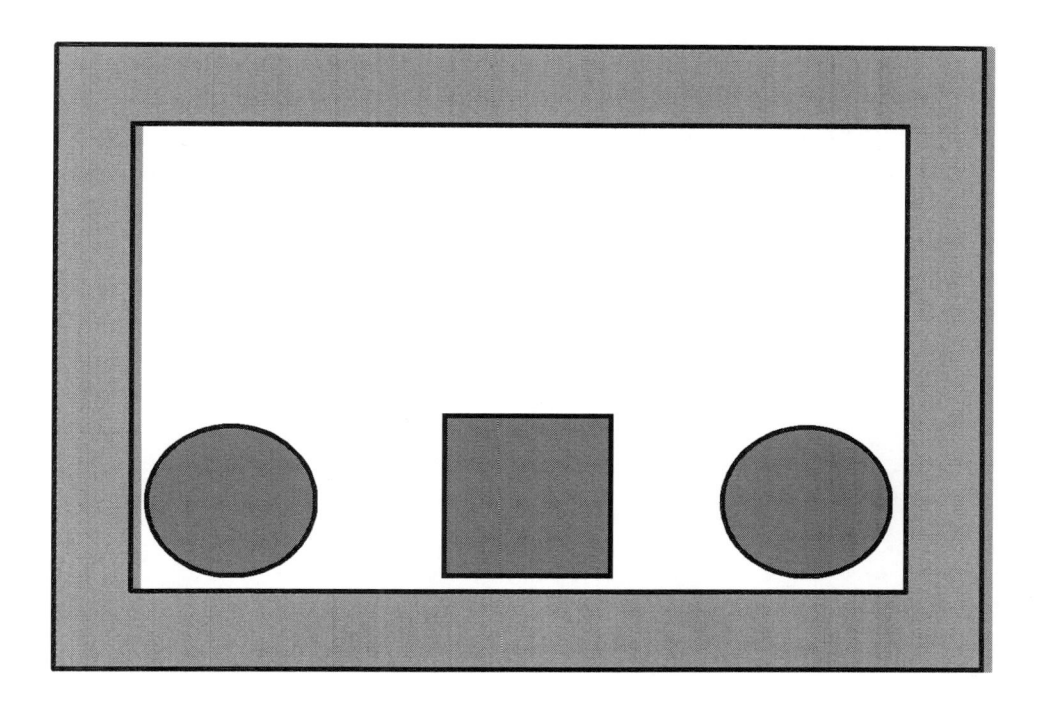

Activity 2

1. Select a square and two circles.
2. Place a circle in the bottom left corner of the box.
3. Place the other circle in the bottom right corner of the box.
4. Place the square between the two circles.

Working Memory Boxes

Intermediate Level

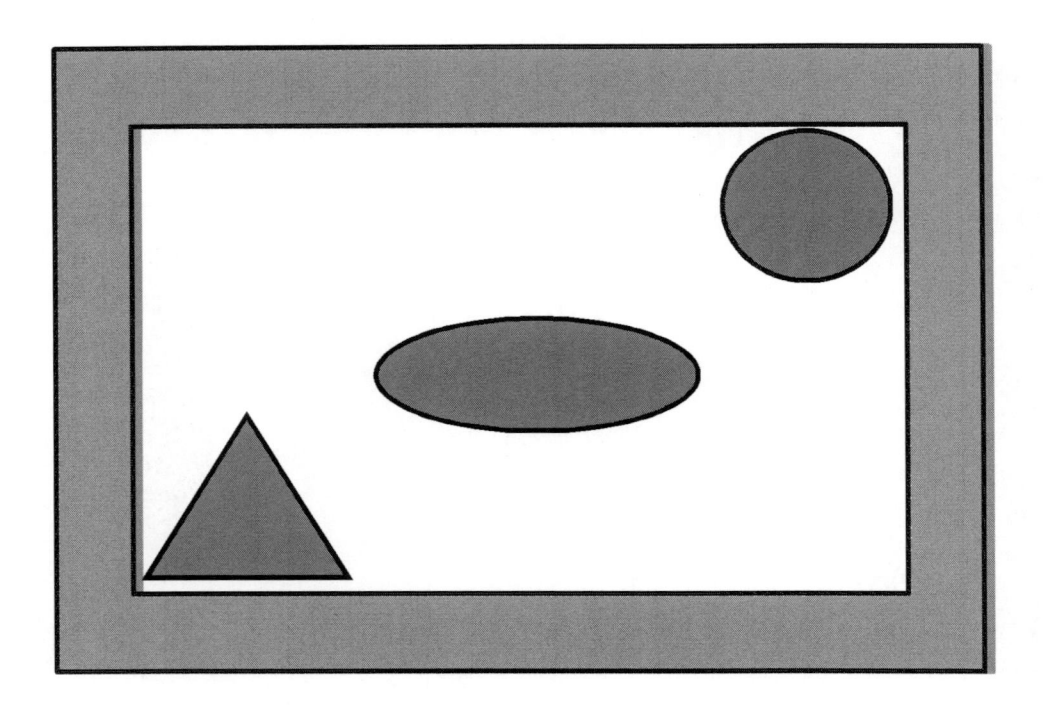

Activity 3

1. Select a triangle, a circle and an oval.
2. Place the circle in the top right corner of the box.
3. Place the triangle in the bottom left corner of the box.
4. Place the oval between the circle and the triangle on its side.

Working Memory Boxes

Intermediate Level

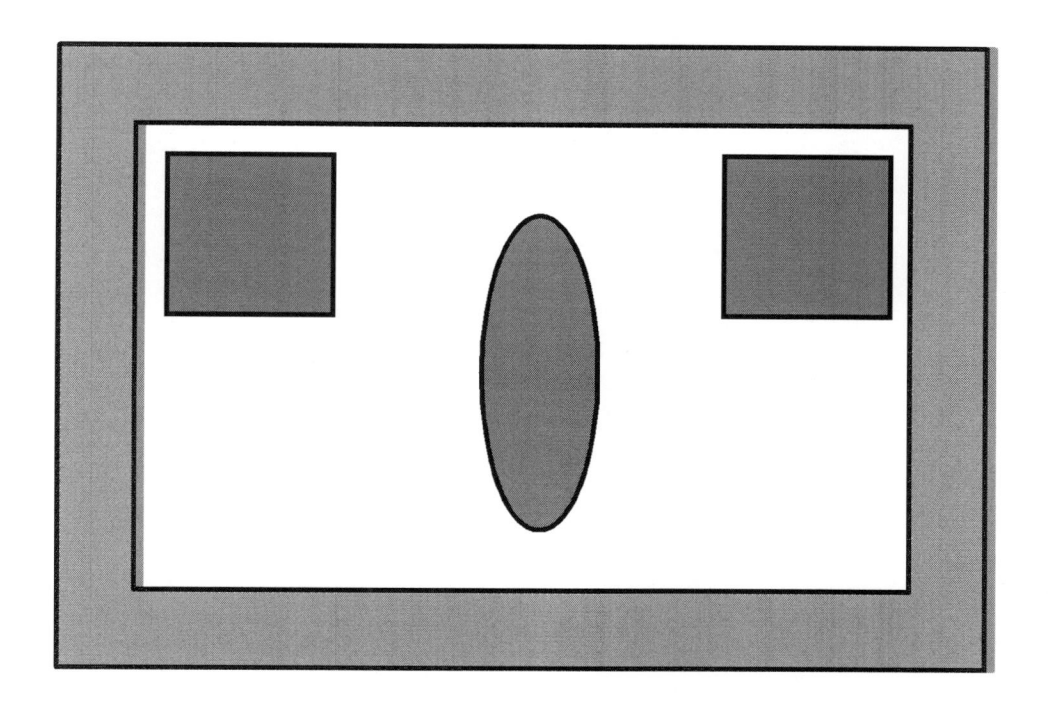

Activity 4

1. Select an oval and two squares.
2. Place a square in the top left corner of the box.
3. Place the other square opposite the first square in the top right corner of the box.
4. Stand the oval on its end in the middle of the box.

Working Memory Boxes

Intermediate Level

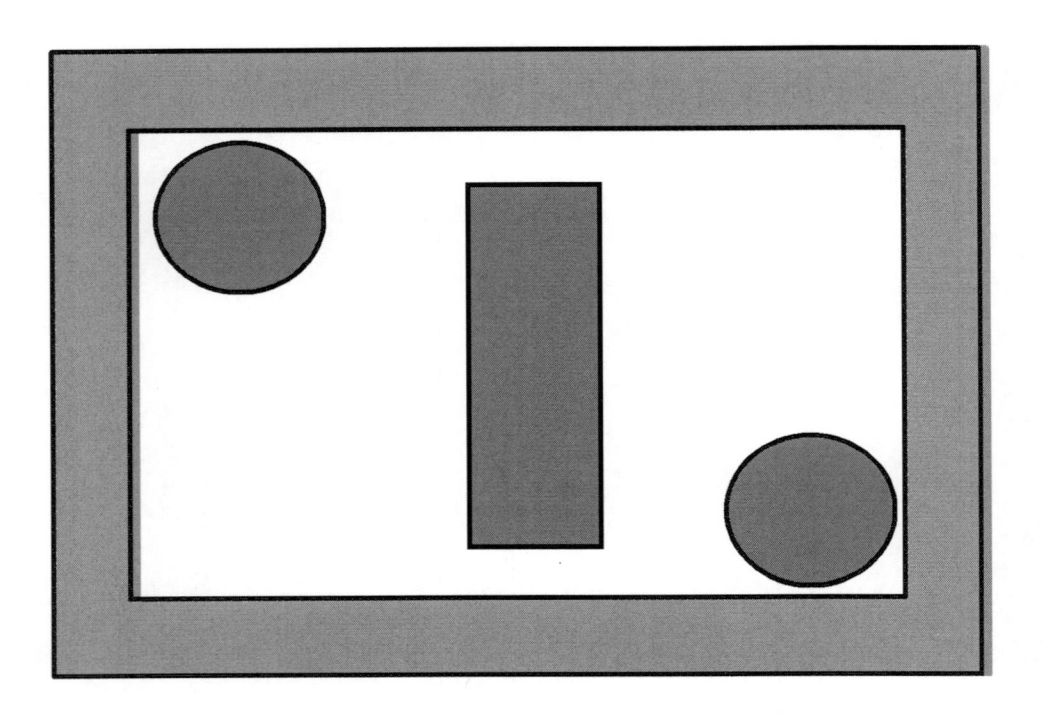

Activity 5

1. Select a rectangle and two circles.
2. Place a circle in the top left corner of the box.
3. Place the other circle in the bottom right corner of the box.
4. Stand the rectangle on its end in the middle of the box.

Working Memory Boxes

Intermediate Level

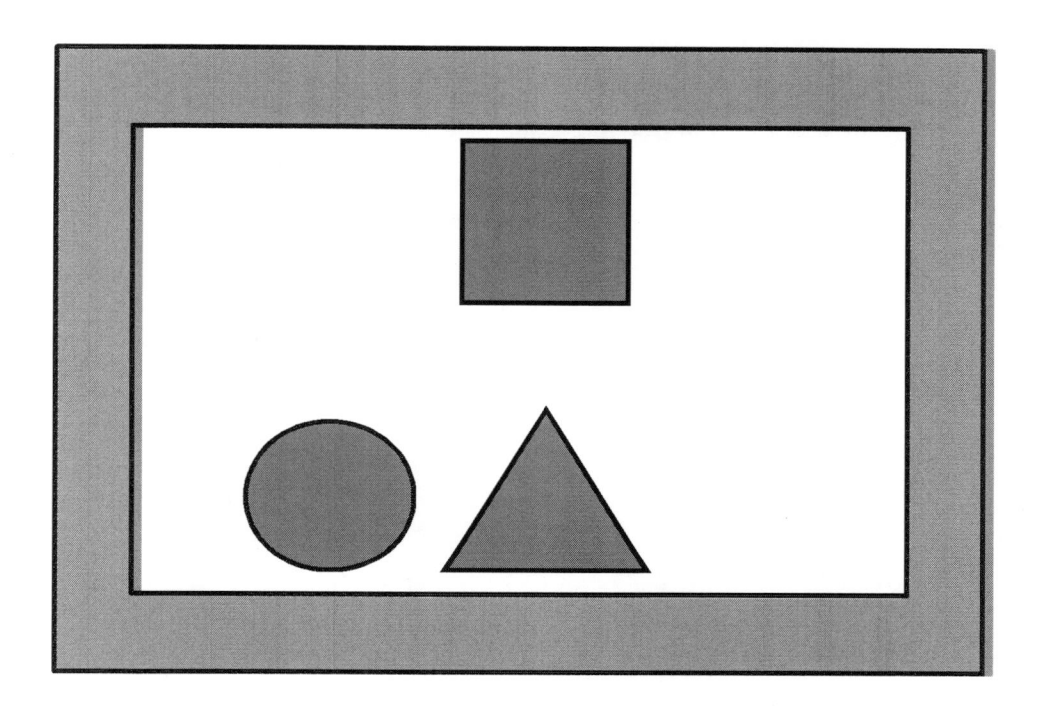

Activity 6

1. Select a circle, a square and a triangle.
2. Place the square at the top of the box in the middle.
3. Place the triangle on the bottom of the box in the middle.
4. Place the circle next to and to the left of the triangle.

Working Memory Boxes

Intermediate Level

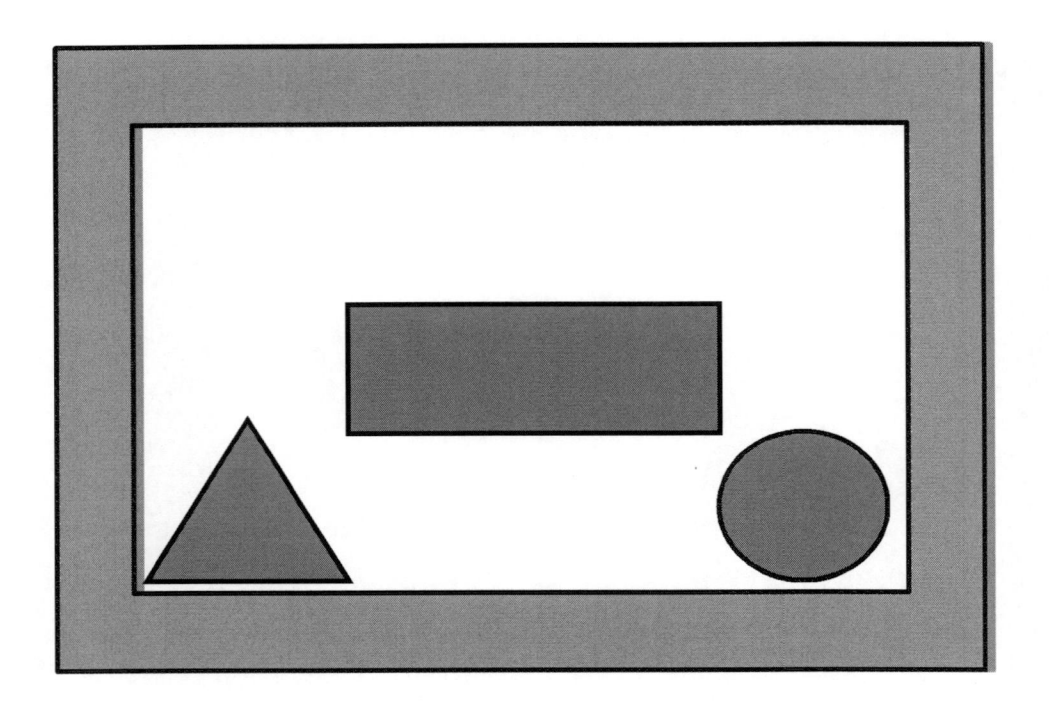

Activity 7

1. Select a circle, a square and a rectangle.//
2. Place the triangle in the bottom left corner of the box.
3. Place the circle in the opposite corner to the triangle on the bottom of the box.
4. Place the rectangle on its side in the middle of the box.

Working Memory Boxes

Intermediate Level

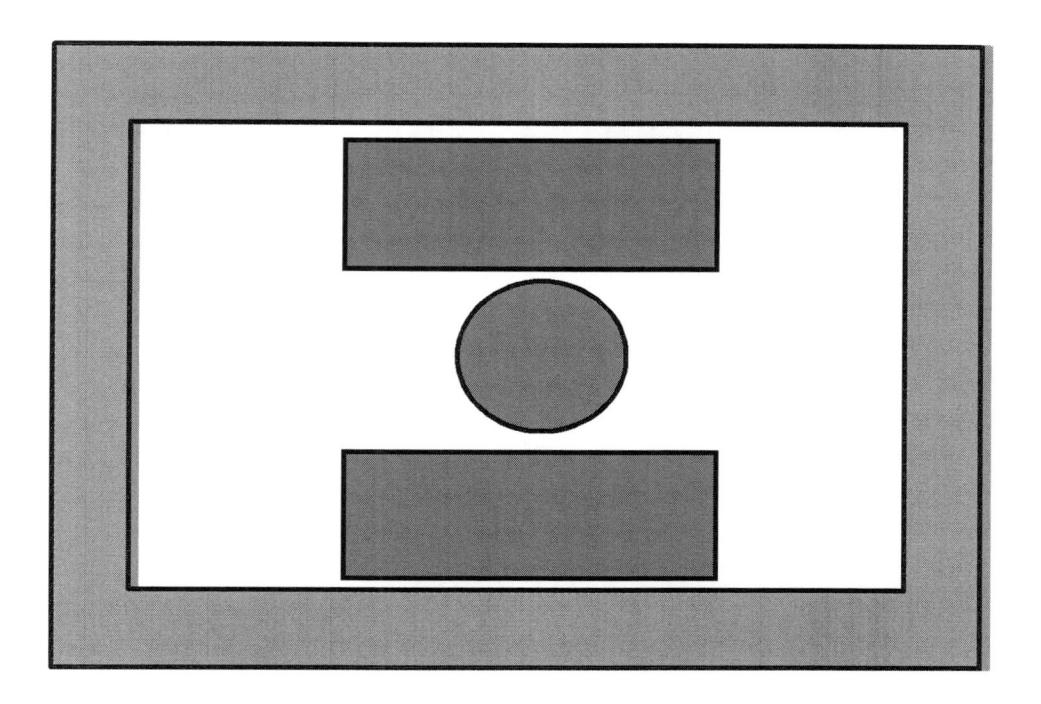

Activity 8

1. Select two rectangles and a circle.
2. Place a rectangle on its side at the top of the box in the middle.
3. Place the other rectangle on its side on the bottom of the box in the centre.
4. Place the circle between the two rectangles in the middle of the box.

Working Memory Boxes

Intermediate Level

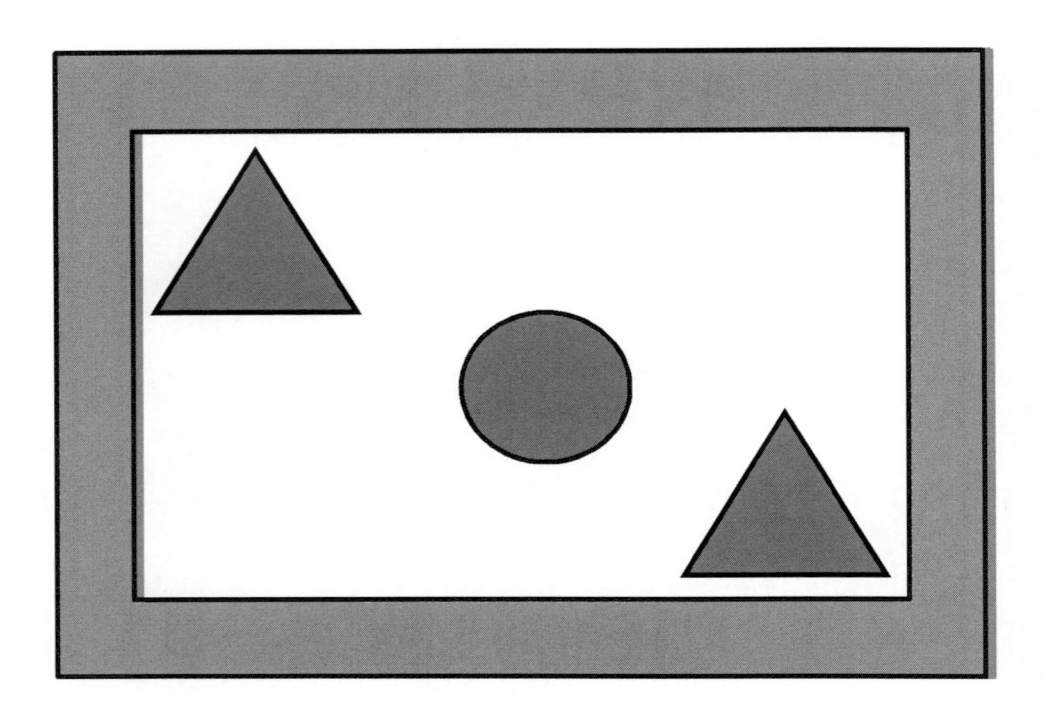

Activity 9

1. Select two triangles and a circle.
2. Place a triangle in the top left corner of the box.
3. Place the other triangle in the bottom right corner of the box.
4. Place the circle between the two triangles in the middle of the box.

Working Memory Boxes

Intermediate Level

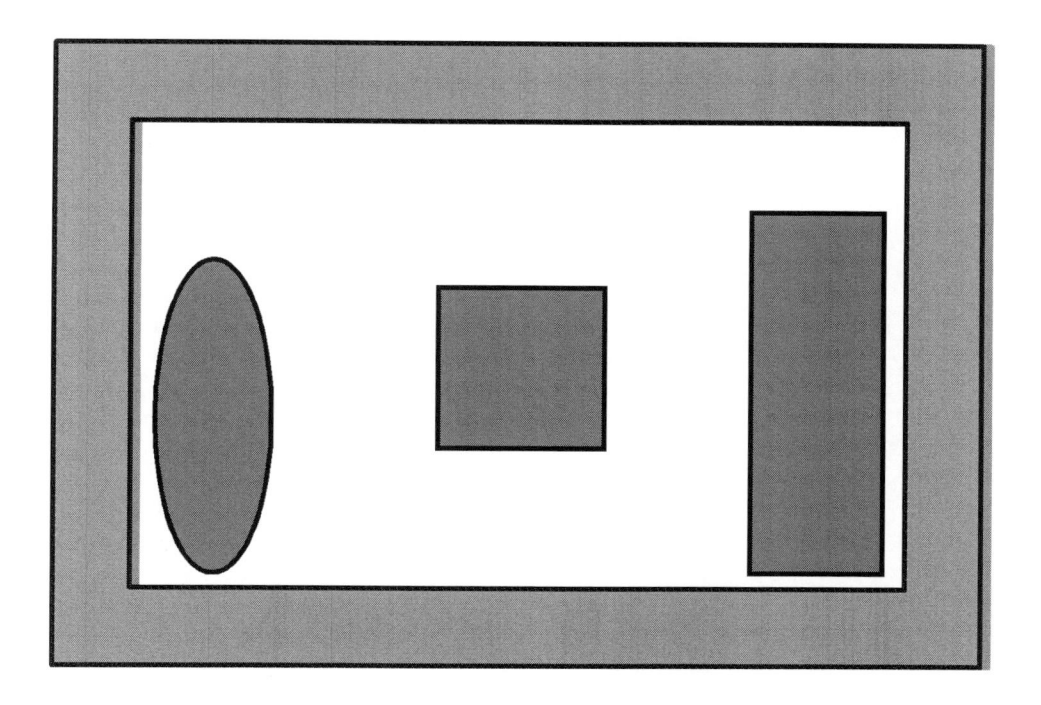

Activity 10

1. Select a rectangle, an oval and a square.
2. Stand the oval on its end in the bottom left corner of the box.
3. Stand the rectangle on its end in the bottom right corner of the box.
4. Place the square in the middle of the box.

Working Memory Boxes

Record Sheet

Tick √ for correct and ✗ for incorrect

Intermediate Level

1. Activty   __ __ __ __

2. Activty   __ __ __ __

3. Activity   __ __ __ __

4. Activity   __ __ __ __

5. Activity   __ __ __ __

6. Activity   __ __ __ __

7. Activity   __ __ __ __

8. Activity   __ __ __ __

9. Activity   __ __ __ __

10. Activity   __ __ __ __

Working Memory Boxes

Advanced Level

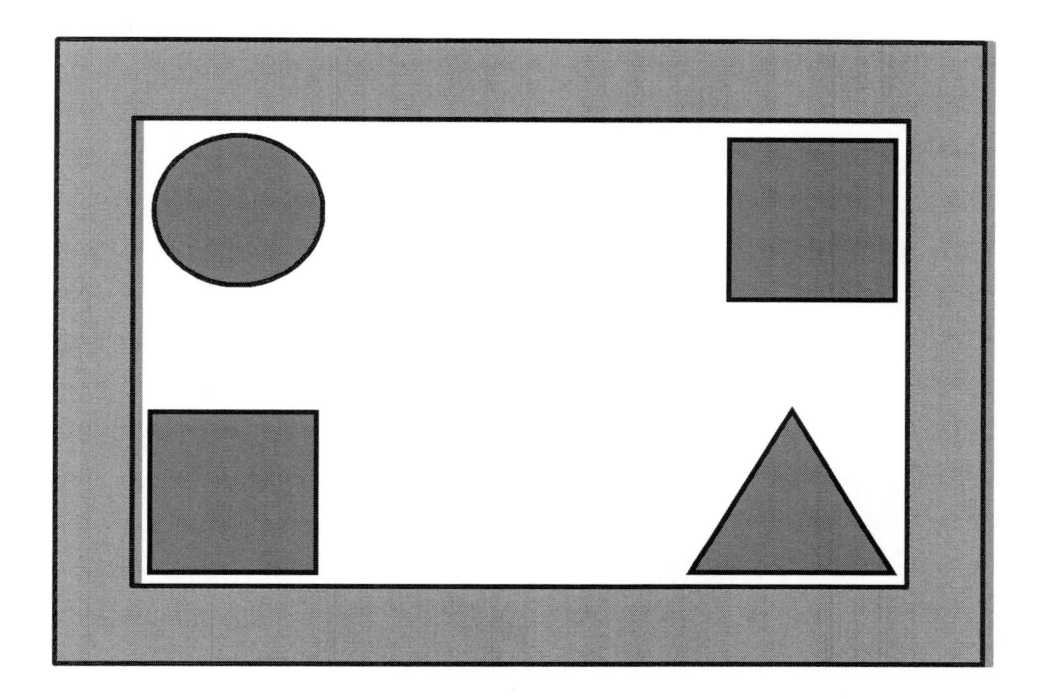

Activity 1

1. Select two squares, a circle and a triangle.
2. Before you place a square in the top right corner, place a triangle in the bottom right corner of the box.
3. Place a square in the bottom left corner of the box.
4. Place a circle opposite and above the square in the top left corner of the box.

Working Memory Boxes

Advanced Level

Activity 2

1. Select two rectangles, a triangle and a circle.
2. Before you stand a rectangle in the bottom right corner, stand a rectangle in the top left corner of the box.
3. Place the circle in the middle of the box.
4. Place the triangle directly beneath the circle.

Working Memory Boxes

Advanced Level

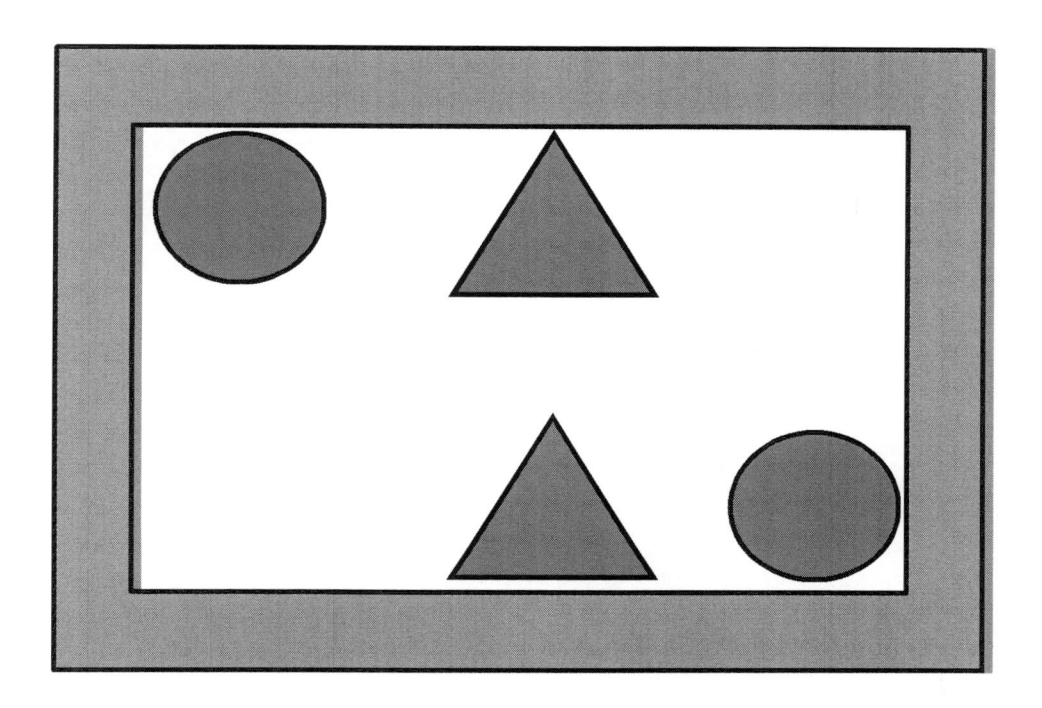

Activity 3

1. Select two triangles and two circles.
2. After you place a circle in the top left corner, place a triangle on the bottom of the box in the middle.
3. Place the remaining circle opposite the first circle in the bottom right corner of the box.
4. Place the remaining triangle directly opposite the first triangle at the top of the box in the middle.

Working Memory Boxes

Advanced Level

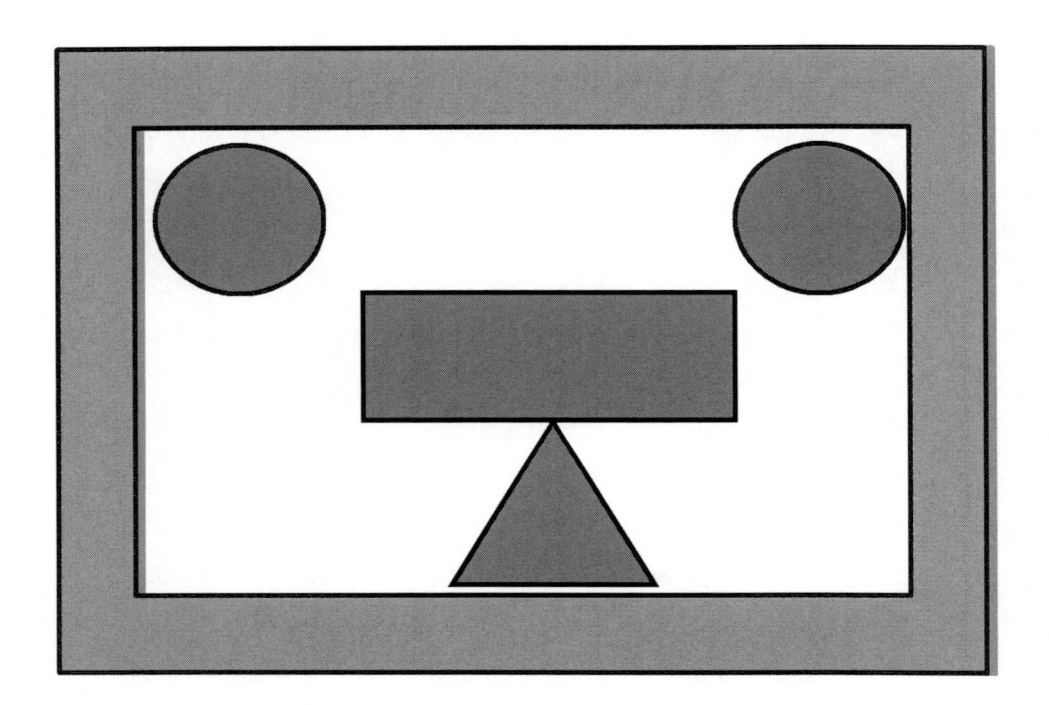

Activity 4

1. Select a triangle, two circles and a rectangle.
2. Place the triangle on the bottom of the box in the middle.
3. Place the rectangle on its side in the middle of the box.
4. After you place a circle in the top right corner of the box, place a circle in the top left corner of the box.

Working Memory Boxes

Advanced Level

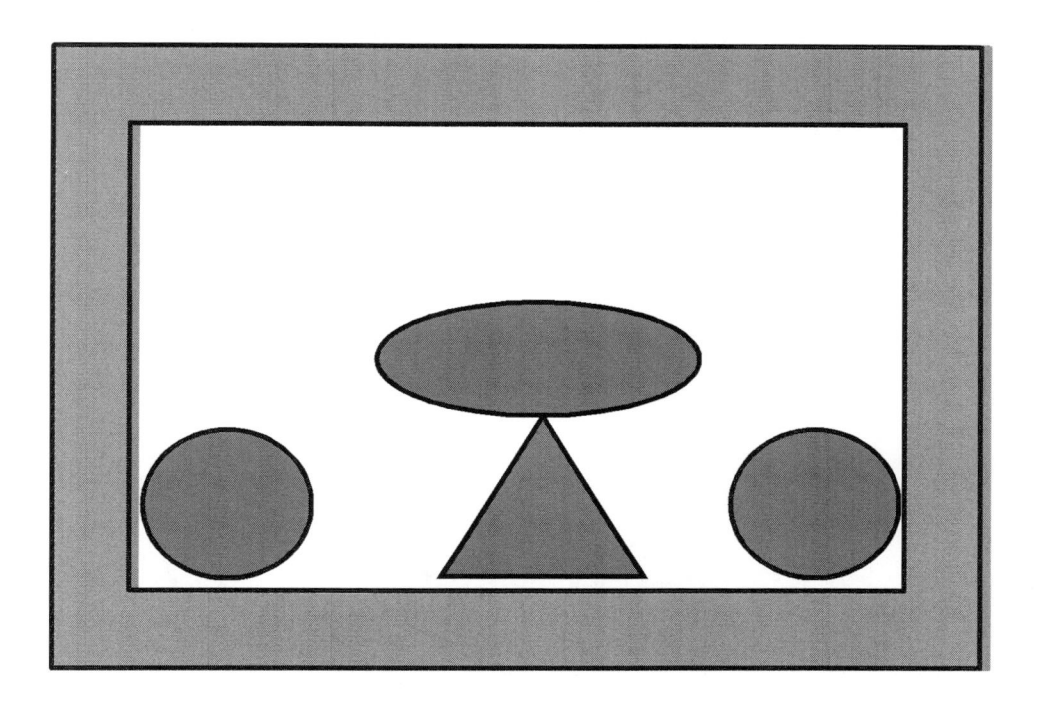

Activity 5

1. Select a triangle, two circles and an oval..
2. Place a circle in the bottom left corner of the box.
3. Place the remaining circle in the bottom right corner of the box.
4. After you place the oval on its side in the middle of the box, place the triangle between the two circles.

Working Memory Boxes

Advanced Level

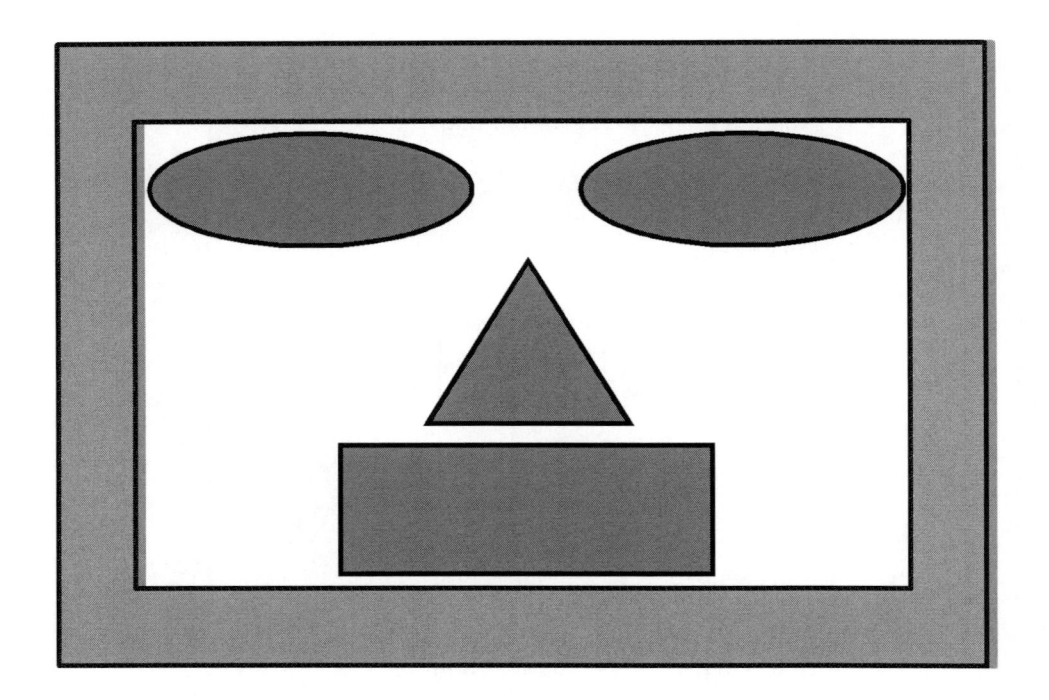

Activity 6

1. Select a triangle, two ovals and a rectangle.
2. Place the triangle in the centre of the box.
3. Before you place an oval on its side in the top left corner, place the rectangle on its side on the bottom of the box in the middle.
4. Place the remaining oval on its side in the top right corner of the box.

Working Memory Boxes

Advanced Level

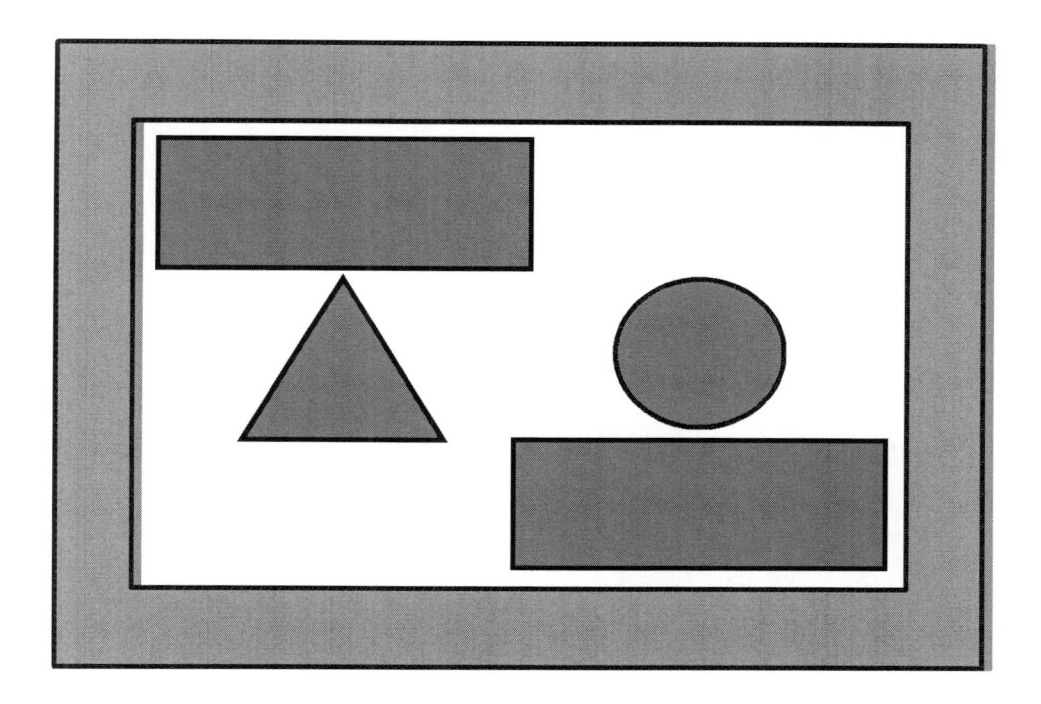

Activity 7

1. Select two rectangles, a triangle and a circle.
2. Before you place a rectangle on its side in the bottom right corner, place a rectangle on its side in the top left corner of the box.
3. Place the triangle directly beneath the top rectangle.
4. Place the circle directly above the bottom rectangle.

Working Memory Boxes

Advanced Level

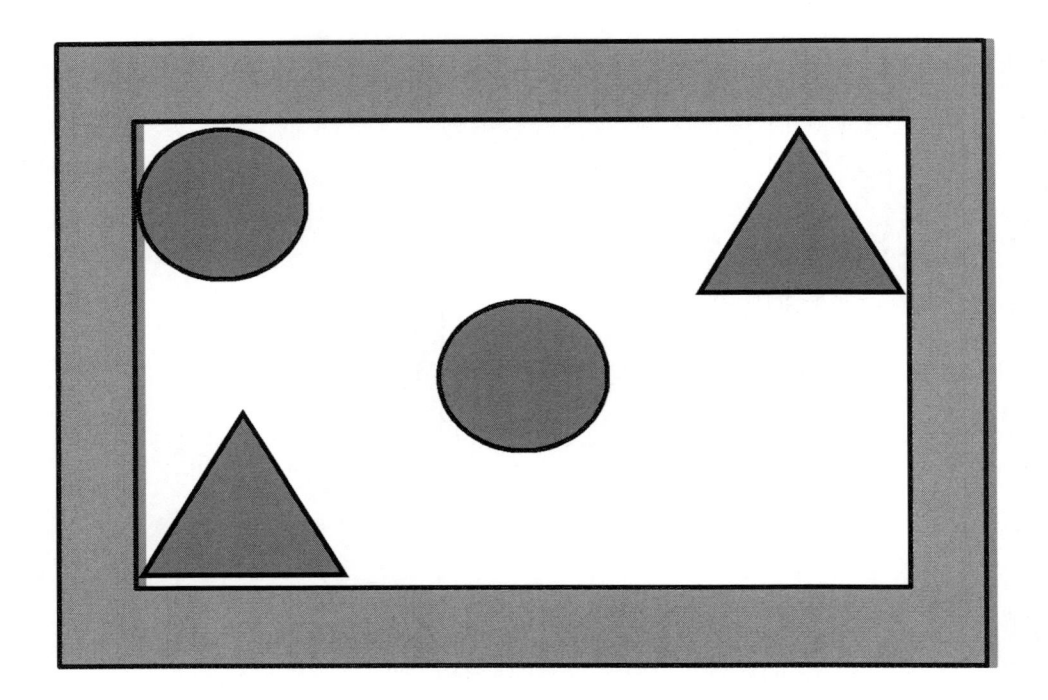

Activity 8

1. Select two triangles and two circles.

2. Place a circle in the top left corner of the box.

3. After you place a triangle in the bottom left corner, place a triangle in the top right corner of the box.

4. Place the remaining circle between the two triangles.

Working Memory Boxes

Advanced Level

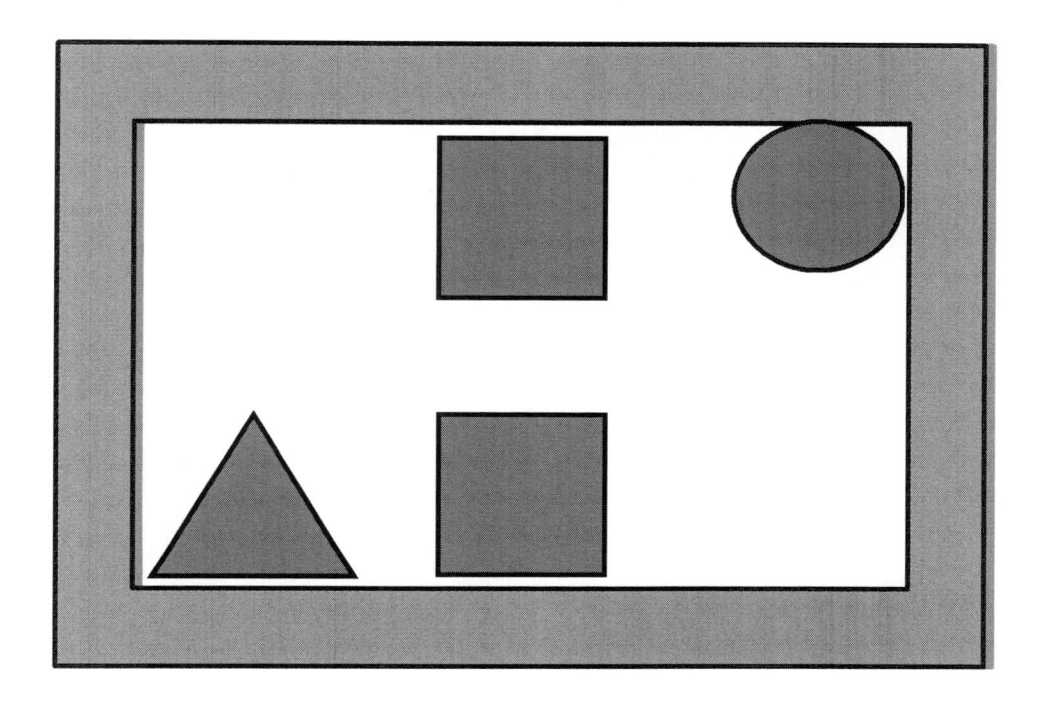

Activity 9

1. Select two squares, a circle and a triangle.
2. Before you place a square at the top of the box in the middle, place a square on the bottom of the box in the middle.
3. Place the triangle in the bottom left corner of the box.
4. Place the circle in the top right corner of the box.

Working Memory Boxes

Advanced Level

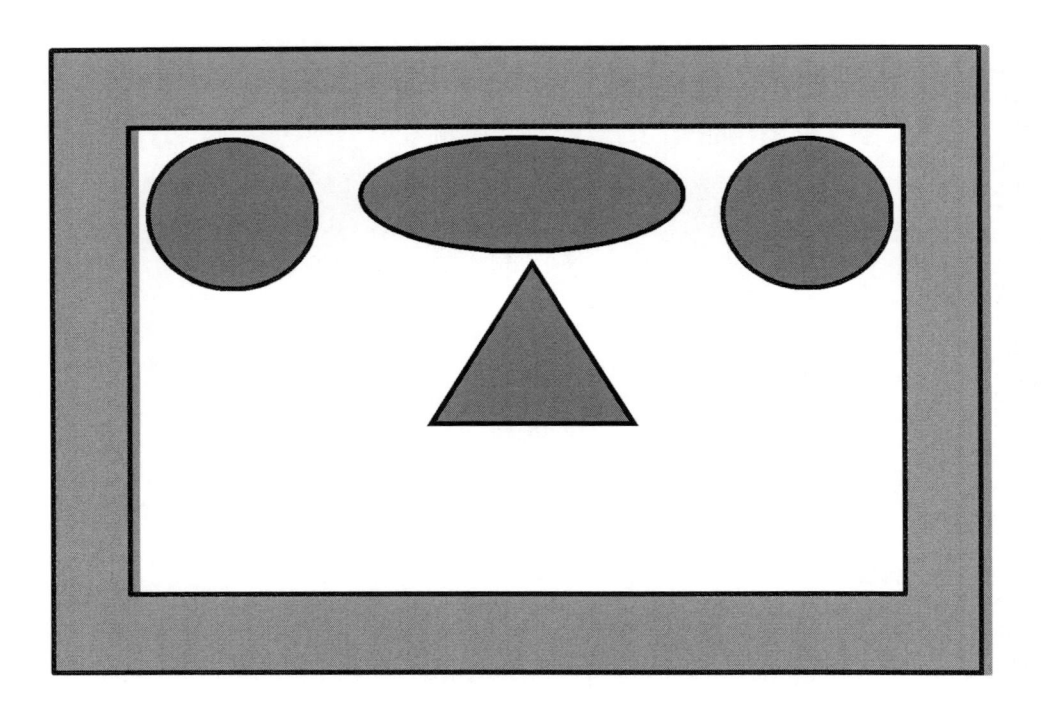

Activity 10

1. Select a triangle, two circles and an oval.
2. Place a circle in the top left corner of the box.
3. Place the remaining circle in the top right corner of the box.
4. After you place the oval on its side between the circles, place the triangle in the middle of the box.

Working Memory Boxes

Record Sheet

Tick √ for correct and ✗ for incorrect

Advanced Level

1. Activity __ __ __ __

2. Activty __ __ __ __

3. Activity __ __ __ __

4. Activity __ __ __ __

5. Activity __ __ __ __

6. Activity __ __ __ __

7. Activity __ __ __ __

8. Activity __ __ __ __

9. Activity __ __ __ __

10. Activity __ __ __ __

Section 7

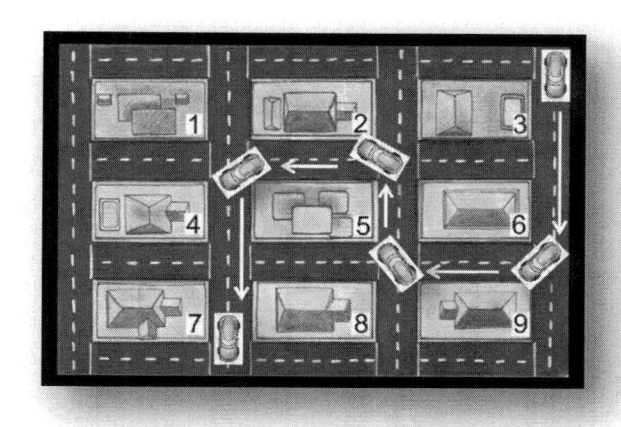

Street Directions

Important: Please note that for **all responses** students may not begin the activity until the clinician has <u>completed</u> the directions.

Working Memory – Street Directions

Instructions

The activities in this section prompt children to follow specific and detailed instructions in order to move a car or motorbike from one location to another.

You will need...

- A photocopied sheet of the street map *(supplied in Appendix A)*
- A top down view car and/or motorbike *(supplied in Appendix A)*
- A left/right orientation marker *(supplied in Appendix A)*
- A custom 50/100 meter ruler *(supplied in Appendix A)*
- A pair of scissors
- A compass *(supplied in Appendix A)*

Cut out and laminate all supplied items. All items can be found in Appendix A or can be downloaded at this web address:

http://www.speechlanguage-resources.com/wm-ex-app.html

Important: It's recommended that children have a clear appreciation that the supplied ruler is set at 50 meters and 100 meters respectively. To use these tools effectively it's recommended that children complete the tutorial before beginning the street directions activity.

Tutorial – *Activity Items*

Introduction to the Street Directions items...

Street Map

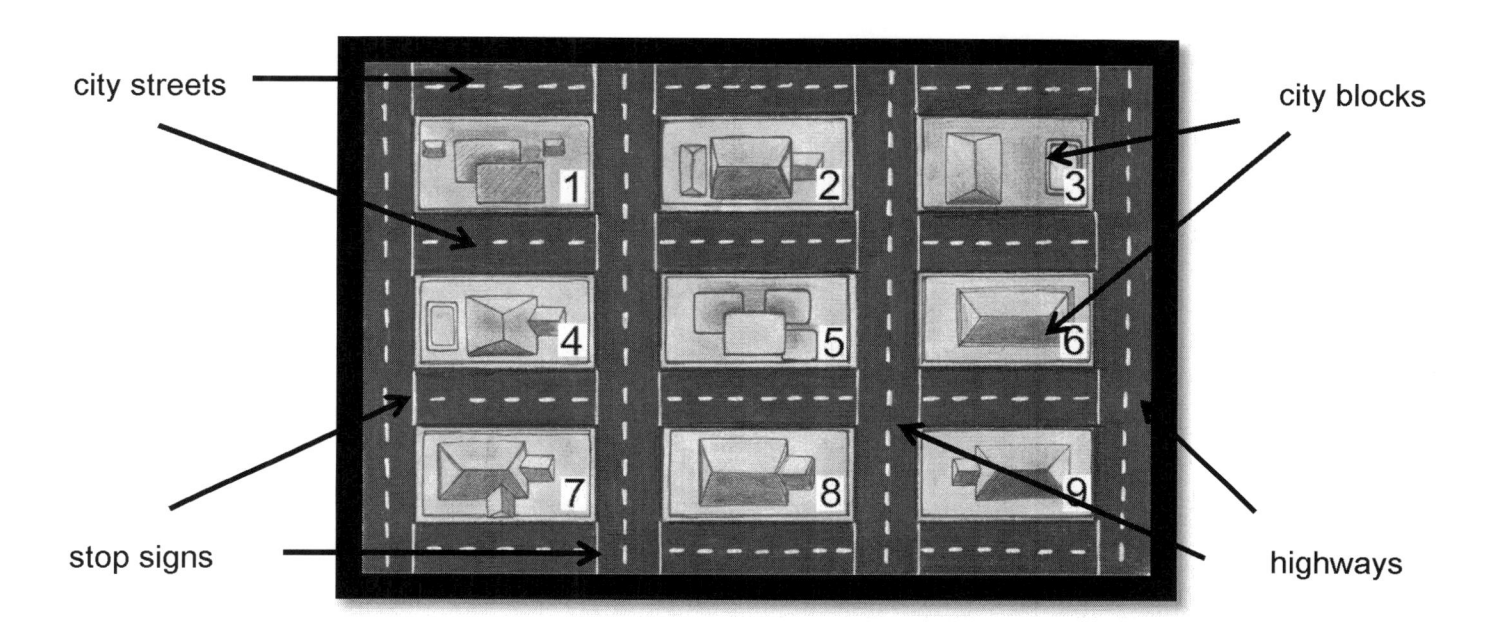

city streets · *city blocks* · *stop signs* · *highways*

The street map is where each player is required to move items such as the car or the motorbike. The street map has nine numbered city blocks. There are four highways and four lots of city streets.

The streets differ from the highways in that there are diagonal lines to represent stop signs. Each player *must* stop at the end of a street before turning left or right.

The A4 photocopy of the sheet can be easily converted to the larger A3 by most photocopiers to enhance game play.

Car and Motorbike

The street directions activity features a top-down view car and motorbike. The vehicles come in different sizes for A4 game-board and A3 game-board use.

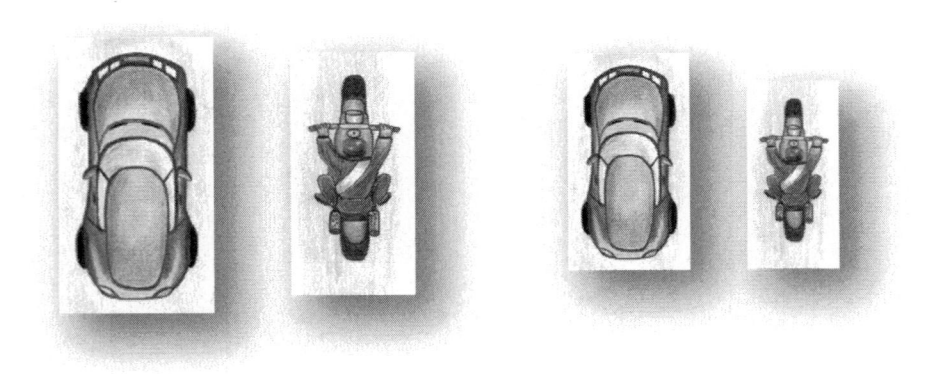

Left/Right Marker

The left/right marker is a visual cue to allow students to correctly orient their vehicles when turning either left or right.

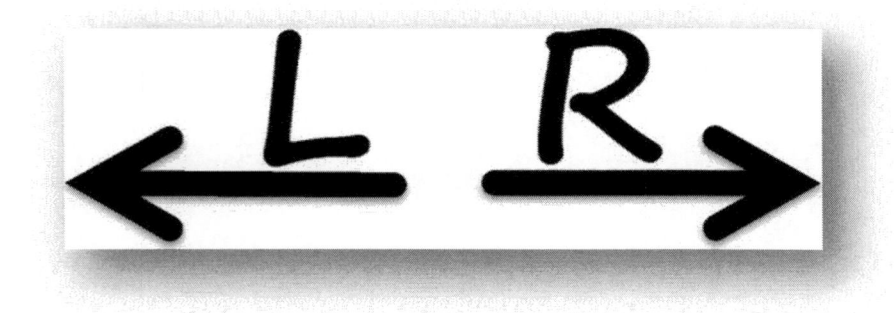

Street Directions – Custom Ruler

The ruler is a guide for students to measure the distance from one location to the next. For simplicity's sake there are only two measures used: 50 meters and 100 meters, which are marked on the card. Of course, these are not real measurements and only work within the context of the activity. There are **two** rulers supplied for the *smaller* **A4** game and for the *larger* **A3** version of the game. **Important:** measure from the *rear* or *backend* of the car or motorbike, never the front.

Correct

Incorrect — *the ruler is too far forward*

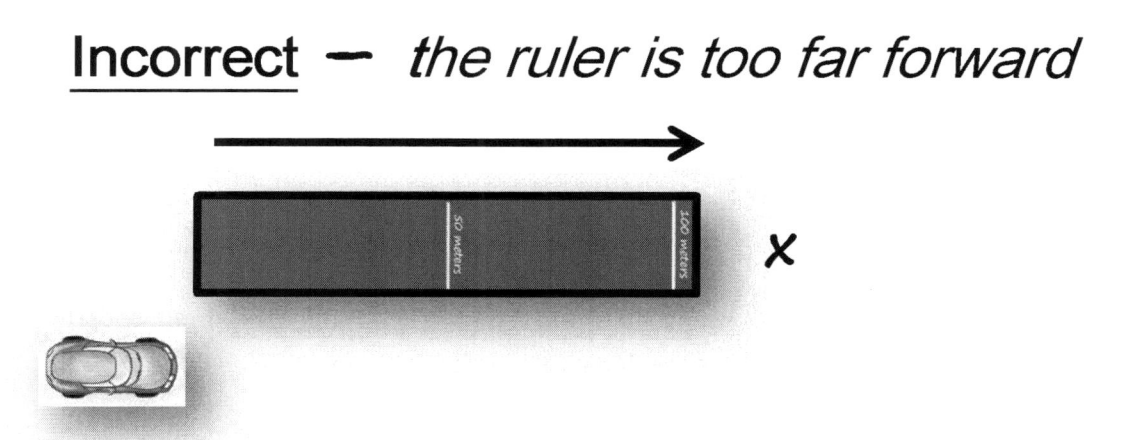

Street Directions – Compass

A compass is a simple device that shows what direction something *is*. The needle on a compass always points *true north*, toward the North Pole. The other main directions on a compass are *east, west* and *south*. *North* is opposite to *south* and *west* is opposite to *east*. For this activity, the compass is a simple means of showing in which direction a vehicle needs to be pointed. Initial instructions will instruct the player to place the car pointing a particular direction such as *north, south, east* or *west*. For instance...

Place the car to the right and below building 9 facing *west*.

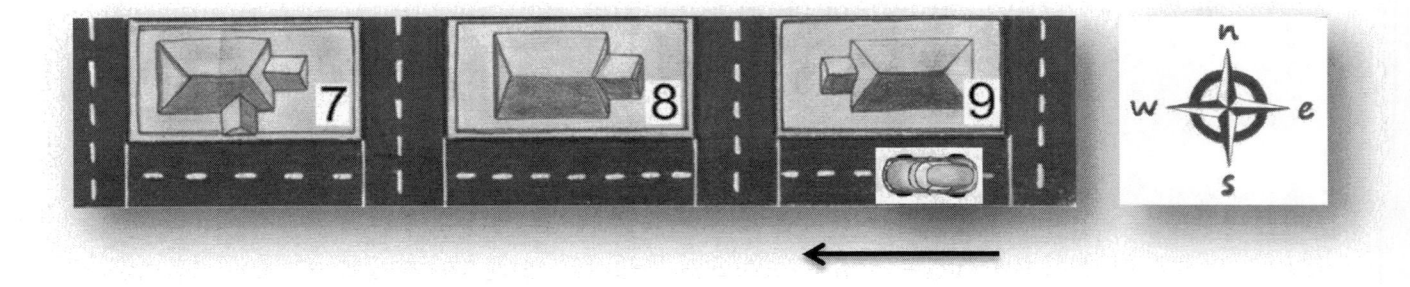

In this example we can see that the car has been correctly placed to the far right of building 9 and *within the context of the activity* is pointing *west*. Encourage students to always position the compass next to the game-board when learning how to correctly place a vehicle.

Working Memory Activities

Tutorial – Street Directions *Example*

This tutorial will demonstrate how to move the car while using the left/right marker and the ruler. In this example scenario the player has been directed to move his car from building 7 to building 5. *The instructions are as follows...*

1. Place the car to the left and below building 7 pointing *east*.

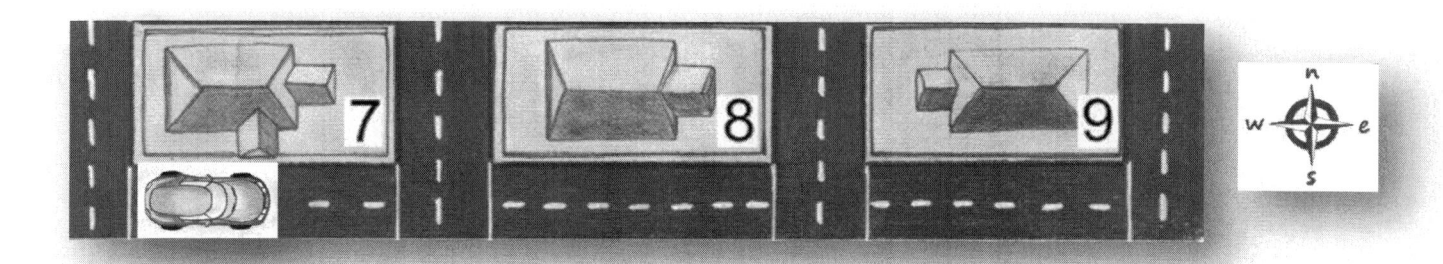

2. Drive to the end of the street and stop.
3. Turn **left** onto the highway and go forward 50 meters.

This is where things can become tricky. To work out left/right encourage the child to place the left/right marker behind the car and orient the car to the *L*, the left.

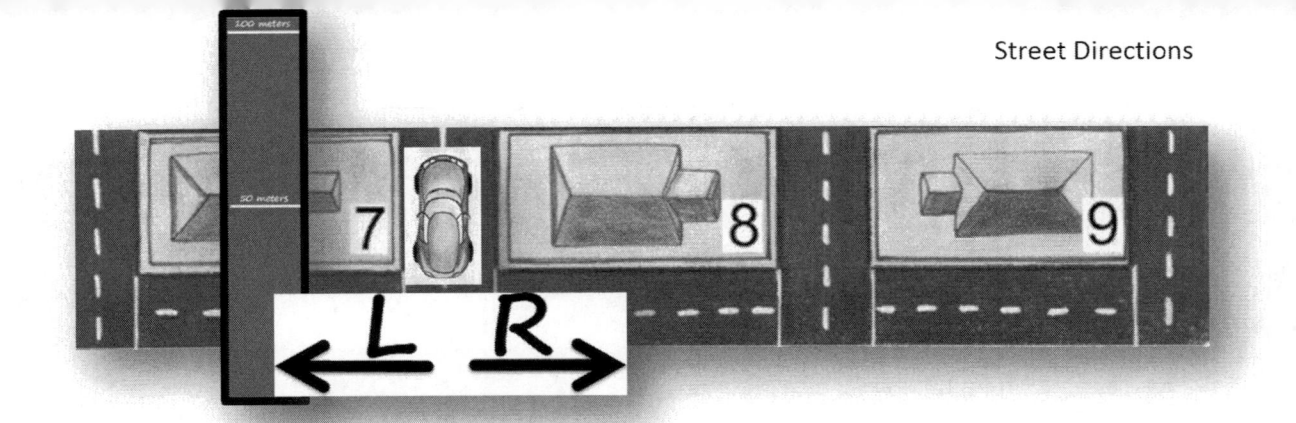

Orient the left/right marker directly *in front* or *behind* the vehicle. This ensures that the child can orient the car in the correct direction so that they don't have to predict left/right in their head, which is an abstract skill that young children find difficult. The ruler is used to measure **50 meters**.

4. Turn **right** into the street and stop at building 5.

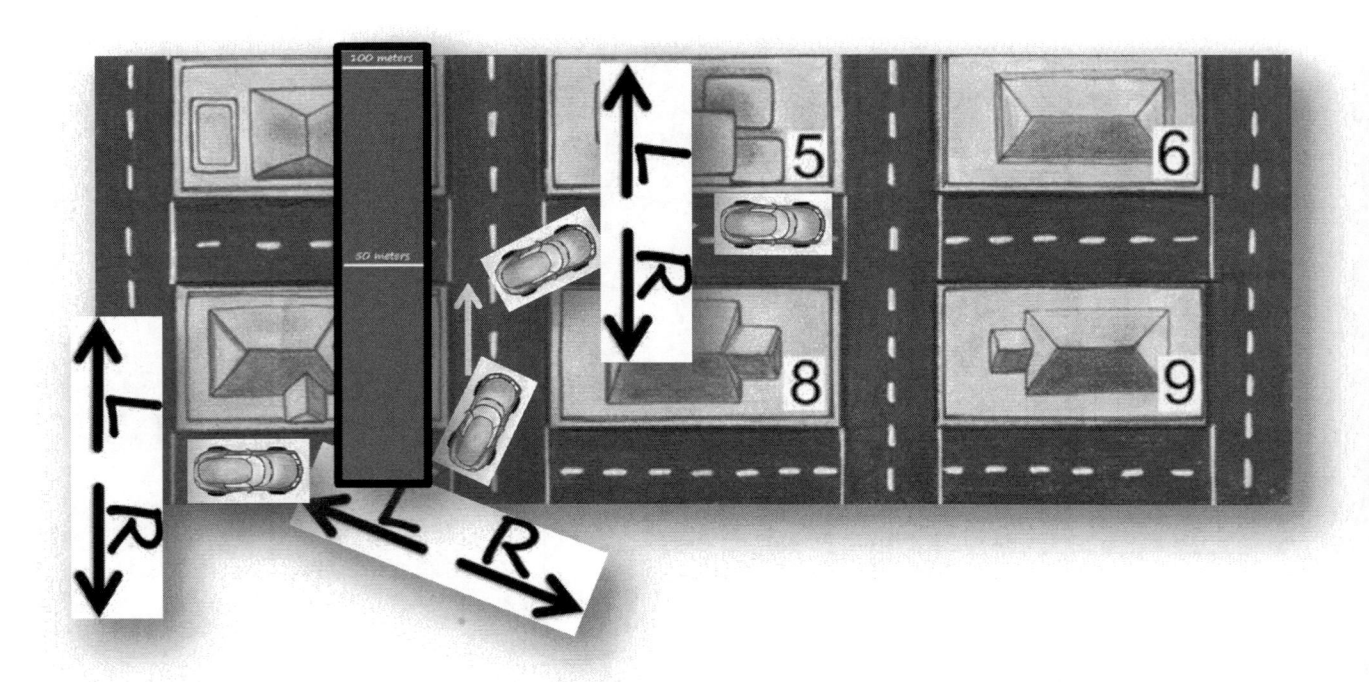

As can be seen from the illustration the left/right marker is always **behind** the car when making a turn.

Working Memory Activities

Working Memory – Street Directions

Activity Layout

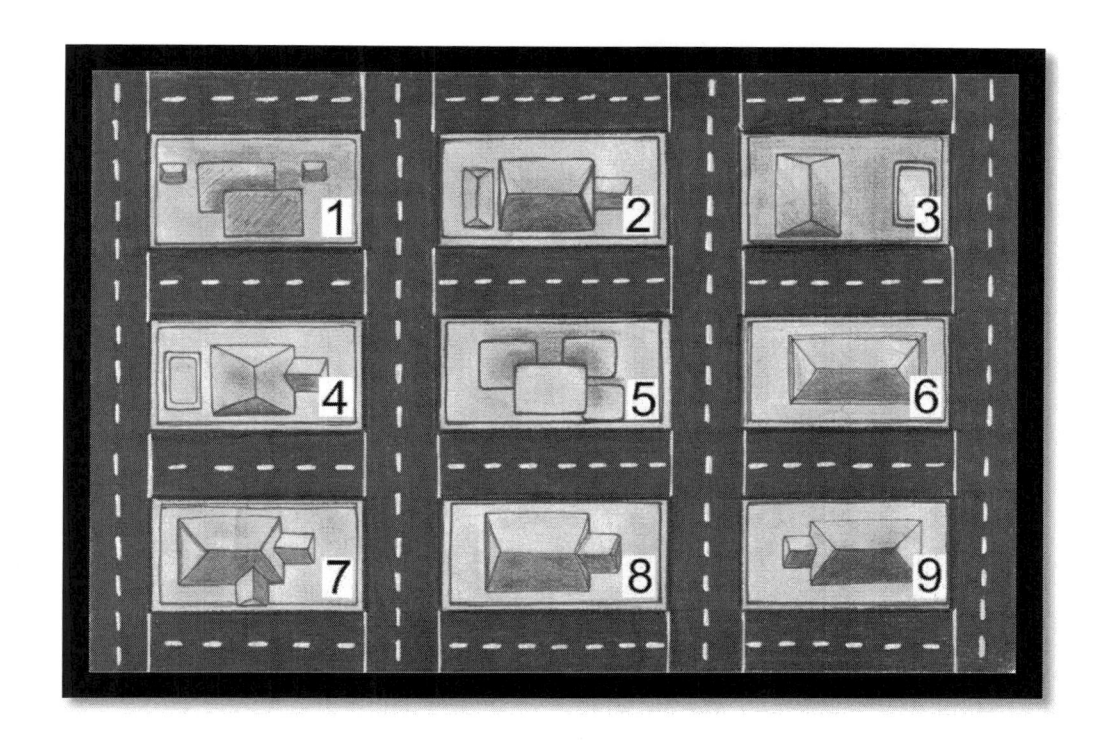

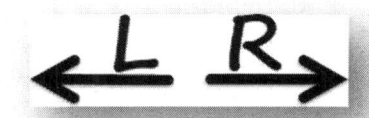

Left/right marker for consistent left/right orientation

Car and motorbike

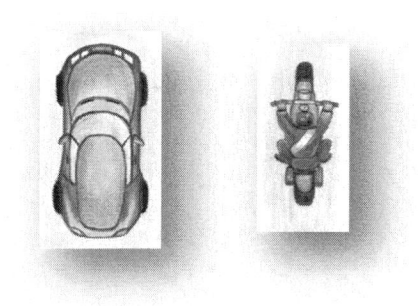

50/100 meter ruler for consistent distances

Compass to assist with correct orientation. Should be placed beside the game-board during play.

Street Directions – Activity Items

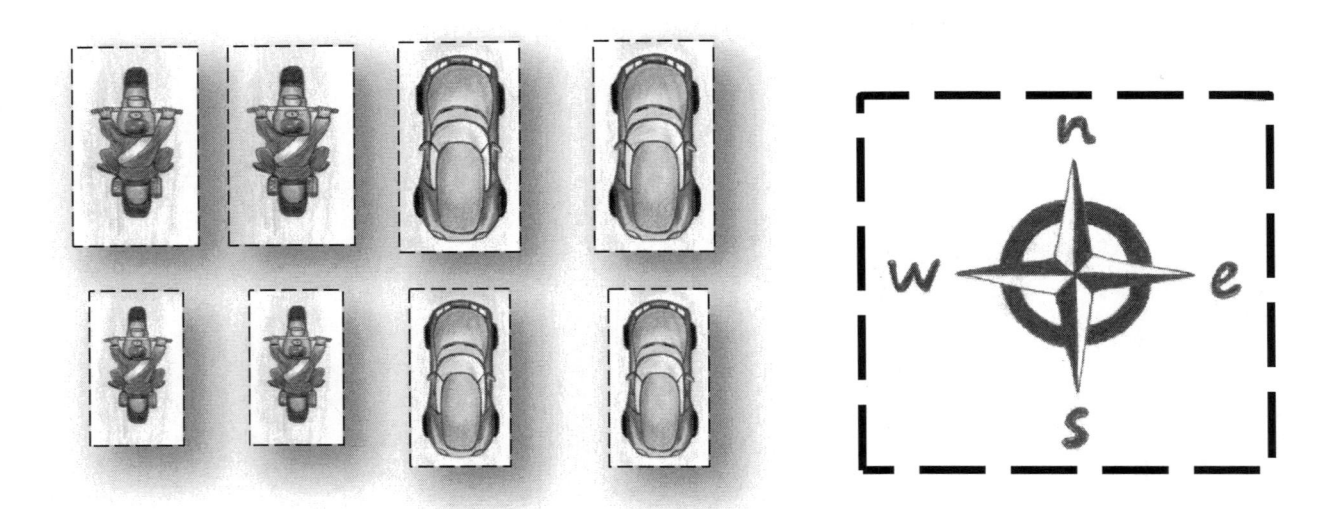

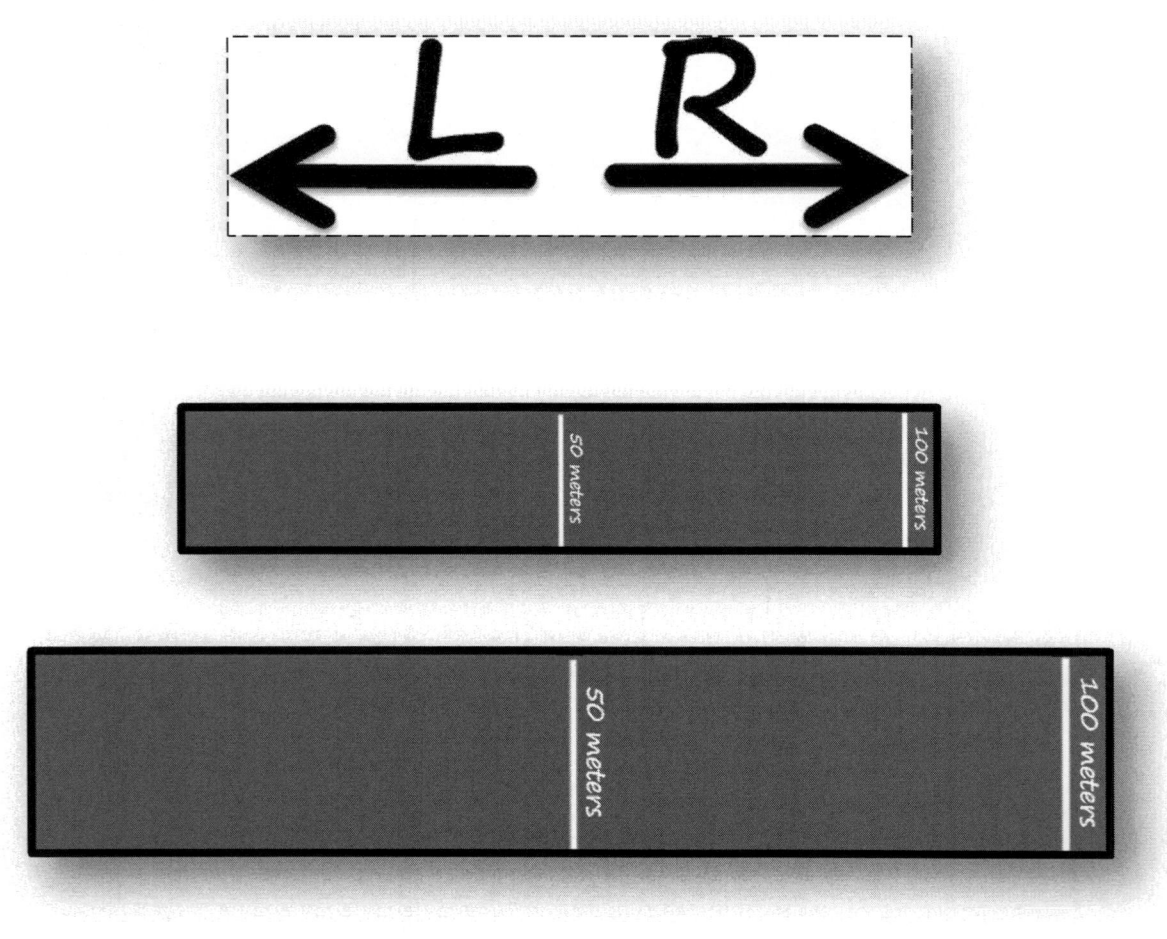

130

Street Map - Directions *Photocopiable*

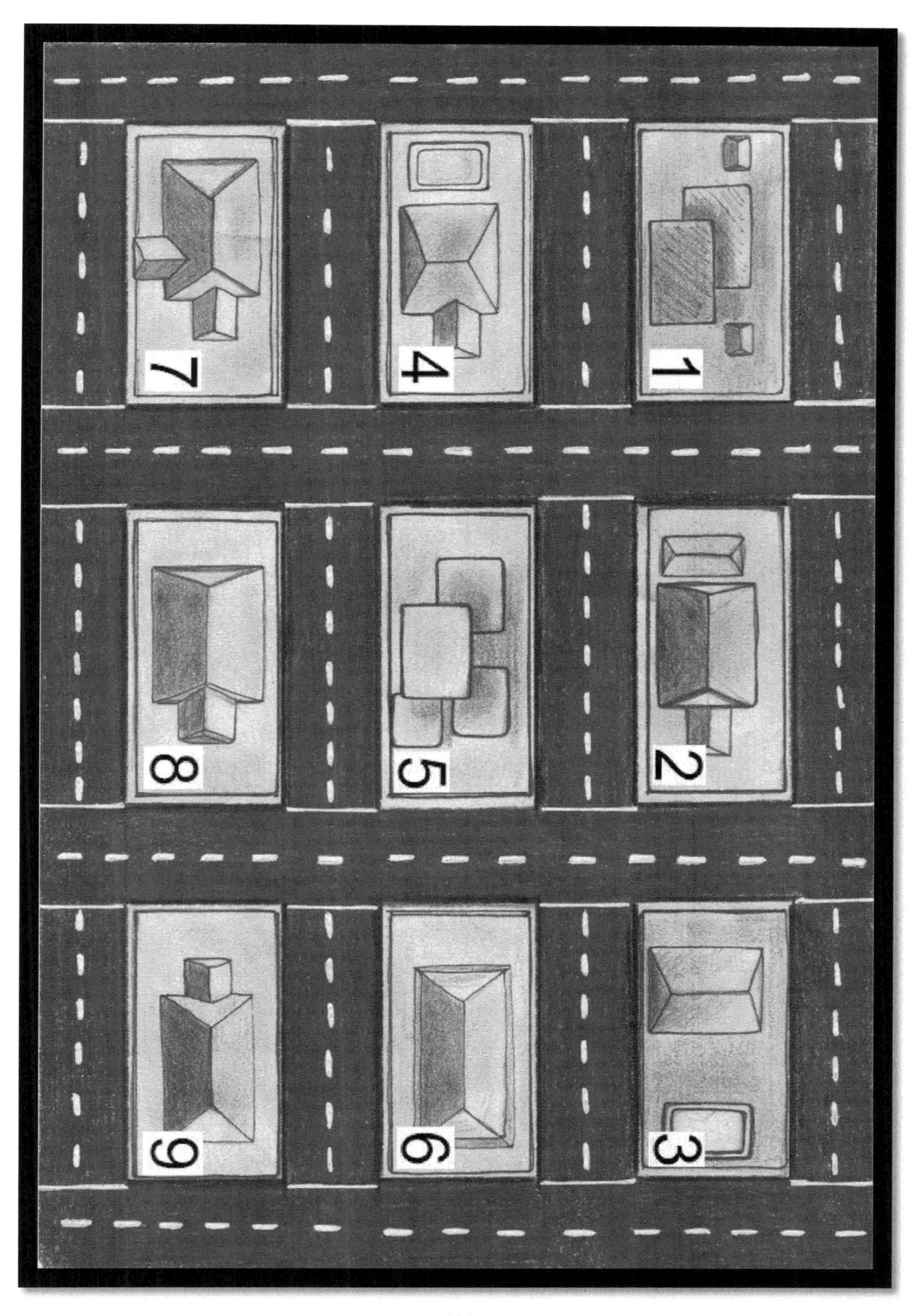

131

Working Memory – Street Directions

Entry Level

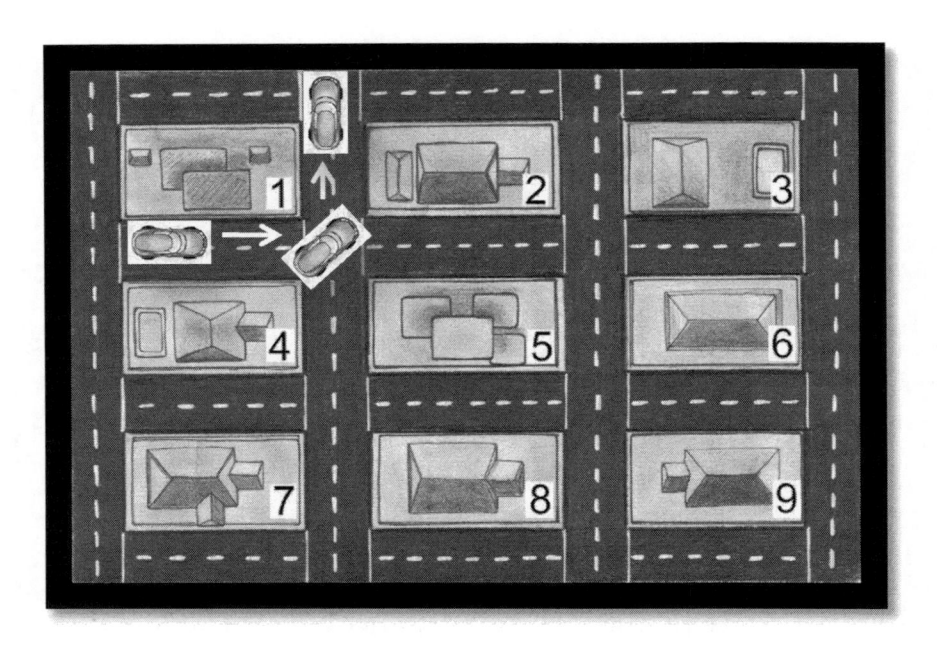

Activity 1

1. Place the car between and to the left of buildings 1 and 4 pointing *east*.
2. Move to the end of the street and stop.
3. Turn left onto the highway.
4. Move forward 50 meters and stop.

(You should be between and slightly above buildings 1 and 2 pointing north)

Working Memory – Street Directions

Entry Level

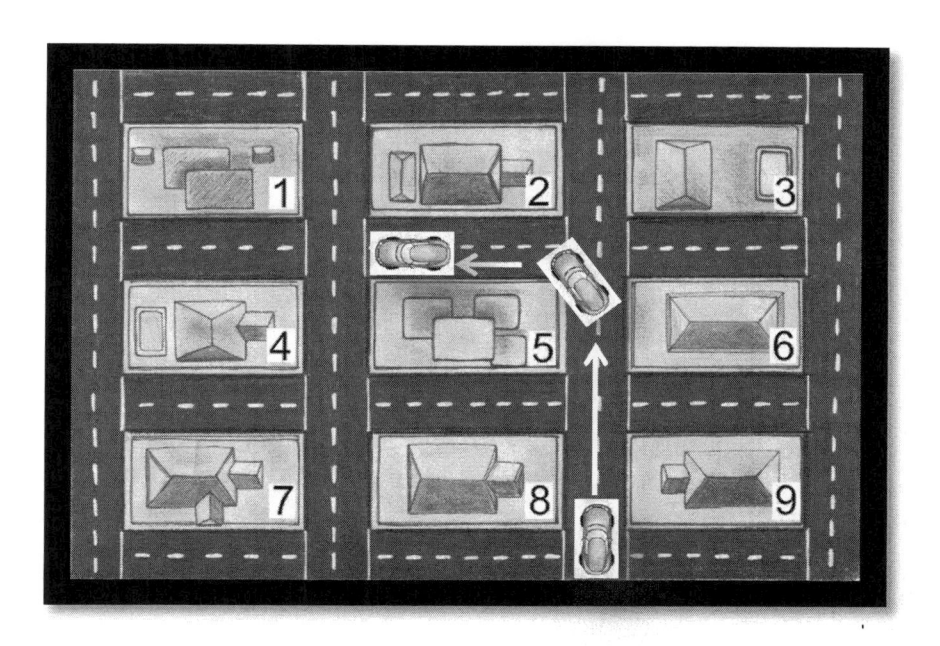

Activity 2

1. Place the car between buildings 8 and 9 at the bottom pointing *north*.
2. Move the car forward 100 meters.
3. Turn left into the street.
4. Move forward to the end of the street and stop.

(You should be between and to the left of buildings 2 and 5 pointing west)

Street Directions

Working Memory – Street Directions

Entry Level

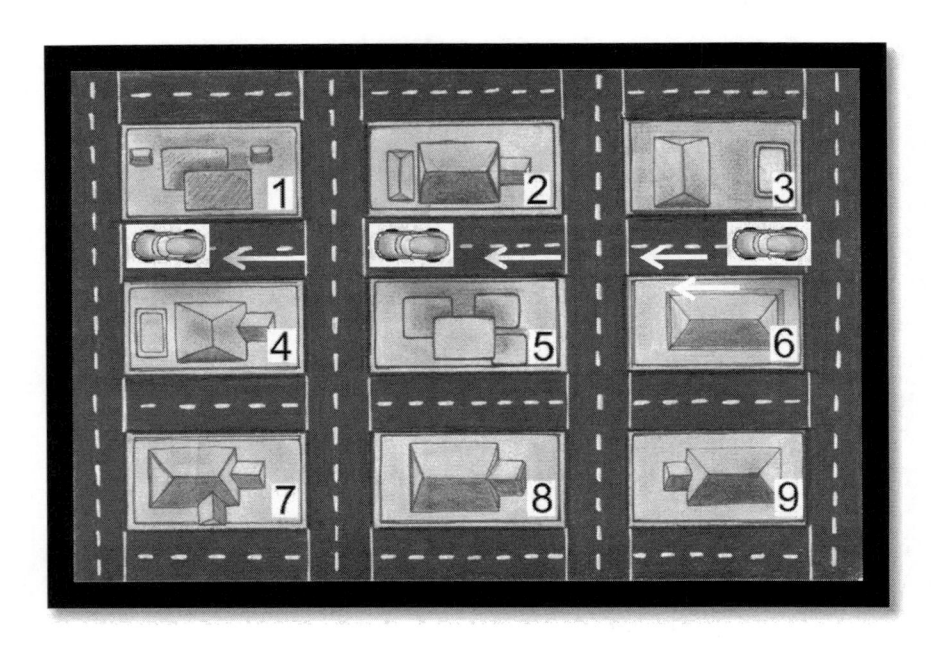

Activity 3

1. Place the car between and to the right of buildings 3 and 6 pointing *west*.
2. Move the car forward to the end of the street and stop.
3. Cross the highway and move to the end of the street and stop.
4. Cross the highway and then stop at the end of the street.

(You should be between and to the left of buildings 1 and 4 pointing west)

Working Memory – Street Directions

Entry Level

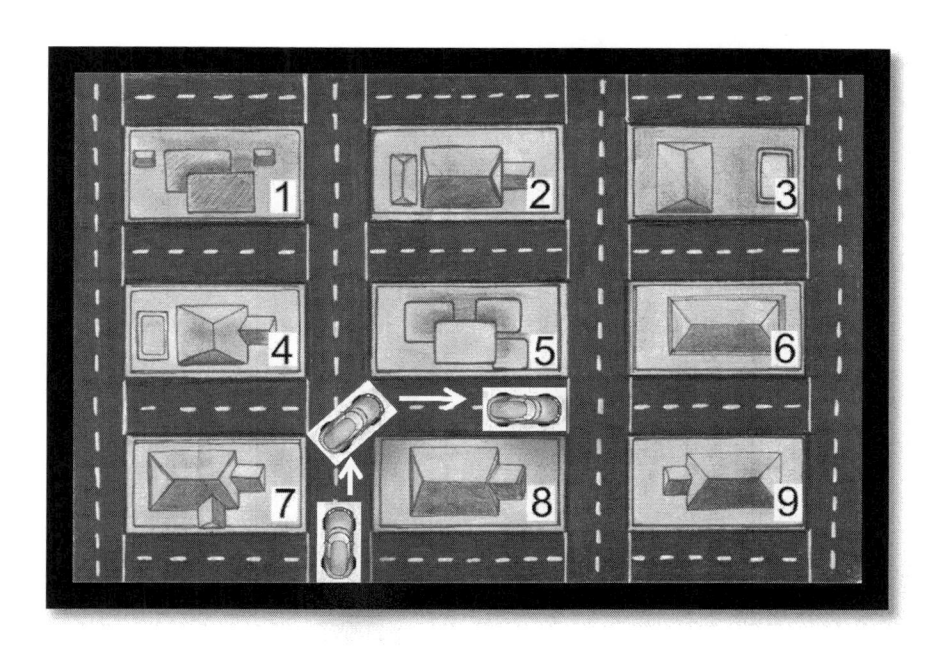

Activity 4

1. Place the car on the highway below and between buildings 7 and 8 pointing *north*.
2. Move the car forward 50 meters.
3. Turn right into the street.
4. Move to the end of the street and stop.

(You should be between and to the right of buildings 5 and 8 pointing east)

Working Memory – Street Directions

Entry Level

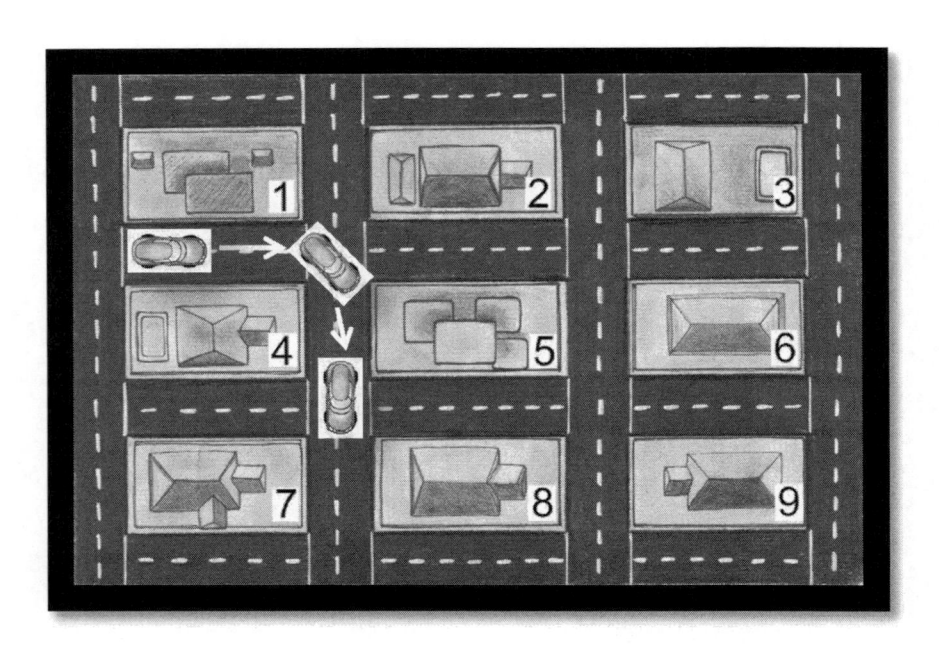

Activity 5

1. Place the car between and to the left of building s 4 and 1 pointing *east*.
2. Move the car forward to the end of the street and stop.
3. Turn right onto the highway.
4. Move the car forward 50 meters and stop.

(You should be between and slightly above buildings 1 and 2, pointing north)

Working Memory – Street Directions

Entry Level

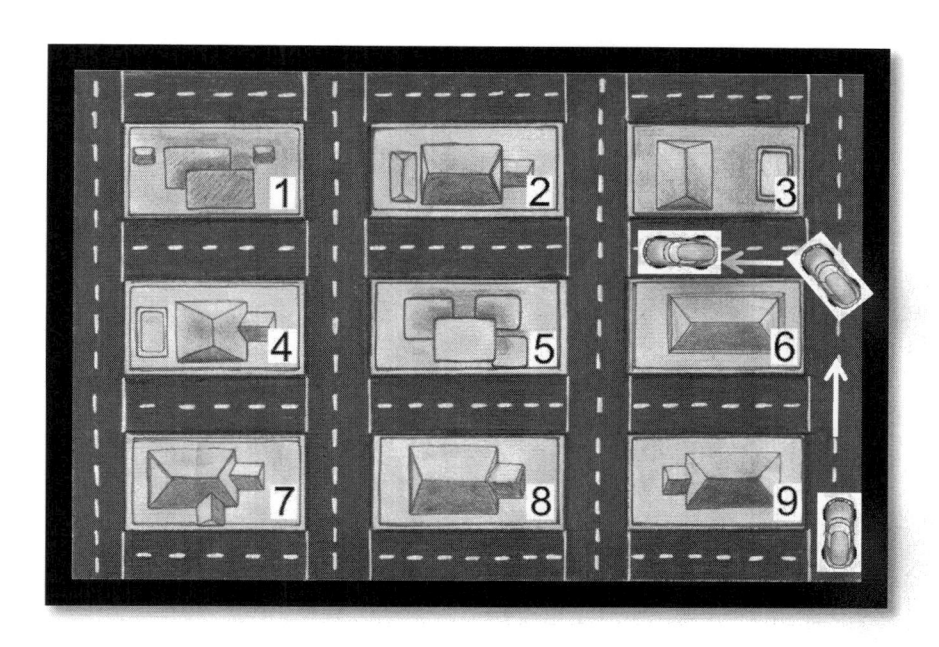

Activity 6

1. Place the car beside and right of building 9 pointing *north*.
2. Move the car forward 100 meters.
3. Turn left into the street.
4. Move the car forward to the end of the street and stop.

(You should be between and to the left of buildings 3 and 6 pointing west)

Street Directions

Working Memory – Street Directions

Entry Level

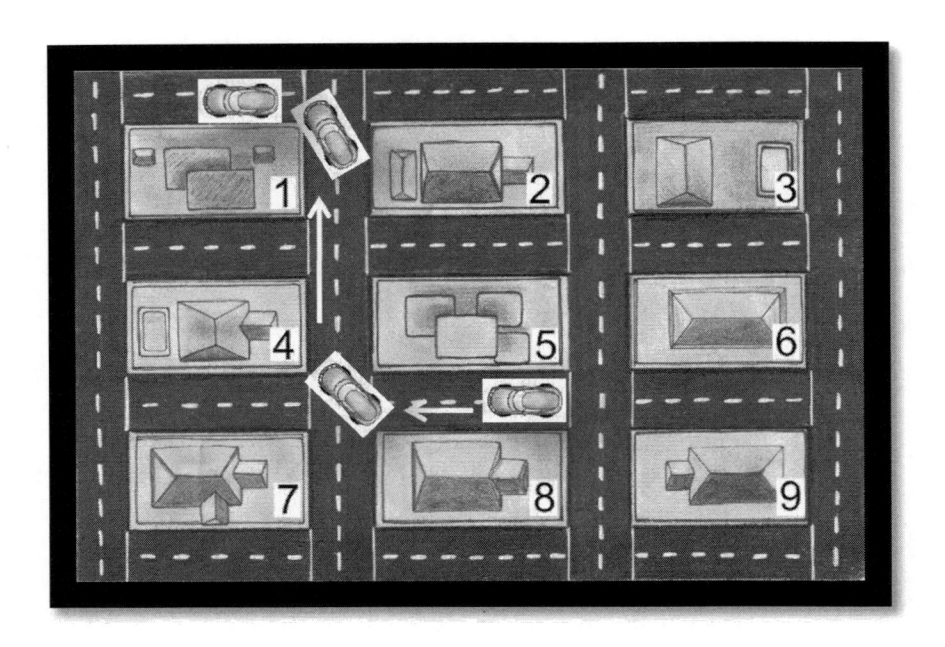

Activity 7

1. Place the car between and to the right of buildings 5 and 8 pointing *west*.
2. Go to the end of the street and then turn right.
3. Move the car forward 100 meters.
4. Turn left into the street and stop.

(You should be above building 1 pointing west)

Working Memory Activities

Working Memory – Street Directions

Entry Level

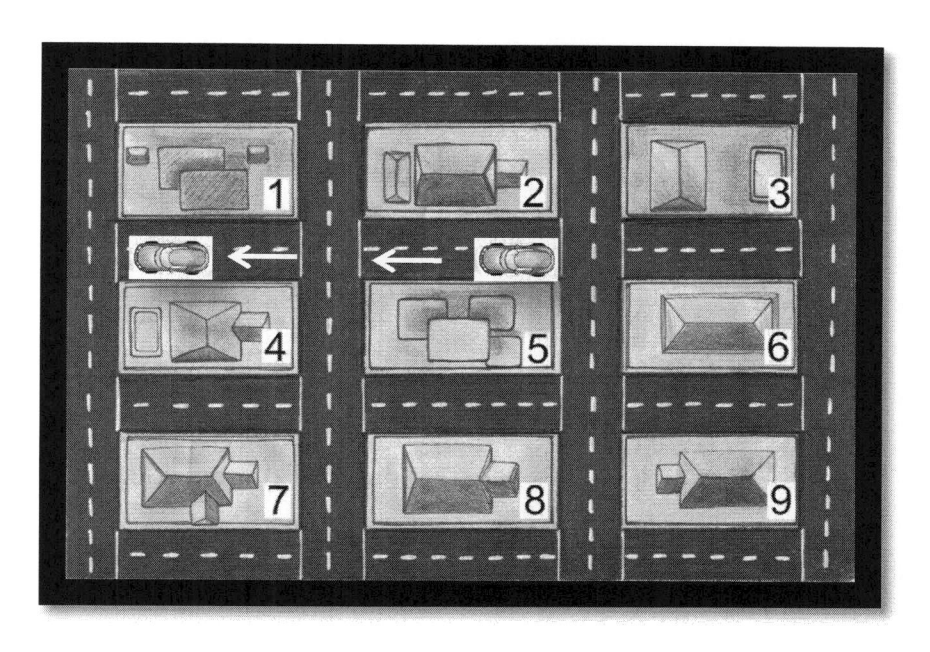

Activity 8

1. Place the car between and to the right of buildings 2 and 5 pointing *west*.
2. Move the car forward to the end of the street and stop.
3. Cross the highway.
4. Move the car forward to the end of the street and stop.

(You should be between and to the left of buildings 1 and 4 pointing west)

Working Memory – Street Directions

Entry Level

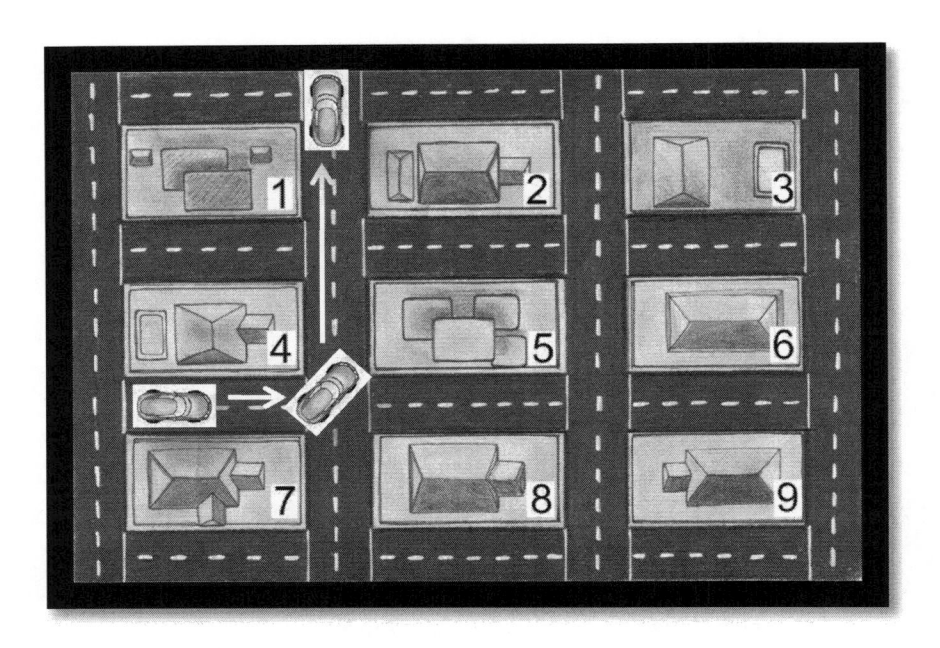

Activity 9

1. Place the car between and to the left of buildings 4 and 7 pointing *east*.

2. Move the car forward to the end of the street and stop.

3. Turn left onto the highway.

4. Move the car forward 100 meters and stop.

(You should be between and slightly above buildings 1 and 2 pointing north)

Working Memory – Street Directions

Entry Level

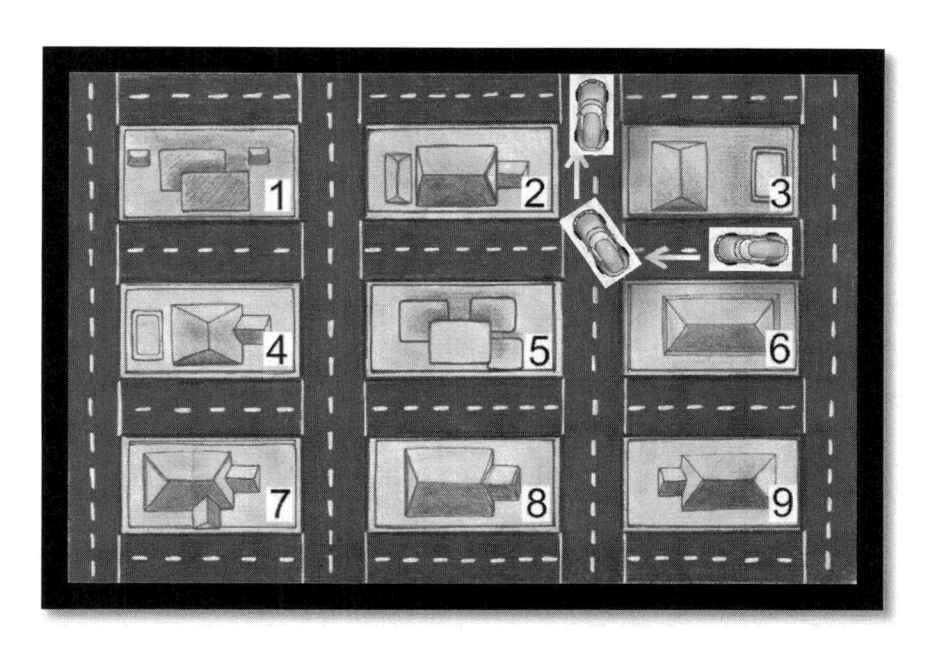

Activity 10

1. Place the car between and to the right of buildings 3 and 6, pointing *west*.
2. Move the car forward to the end of the street and stop.
3. Turn right onto the highway.
4. Move the car forward 50 meters.

(You should be between and above buildings 2 and 3 pointing north)

Working Memory – Street Directions

Record Sheet

Tick √ for correct and ✗ for incorrect

Entry Level

1. Activity   __ __ __ __

2. Activty   __ __ __ __

3. Activity   __ __ __ __

4. Activity   __ __ __ __

5. Activity   __ __ __ __

6. Activity   __ __ __ __

7. Activity   __ __ __ __

8. Activity   __ __ __ __

9. Activity   __ __ __ __

10. Activity __ __ __ __

Working Memory – Street Directions

Intermediate/Advanced Levels

The *intermediate* and *advanced* levels of the **street directions** activity adds extra layers of complexity. The instructions are longer and more difficult. Also, students are required to move their vehicles in ways that can be initially difficult to *visualize*. While playing the entry level activities, students first get to use the **left/right marker** and the **compass** to gauge direction. These tools are vital in the *intermediate* and *advanced* levels of the **street directions** activity.

In the example below, the student turns the vehicle *right* and travels *north* to *south*, or in a sense, *upside down*. To make an accurate turn *left* the student relies on the **left/right marker** to make the correct turn. As before,

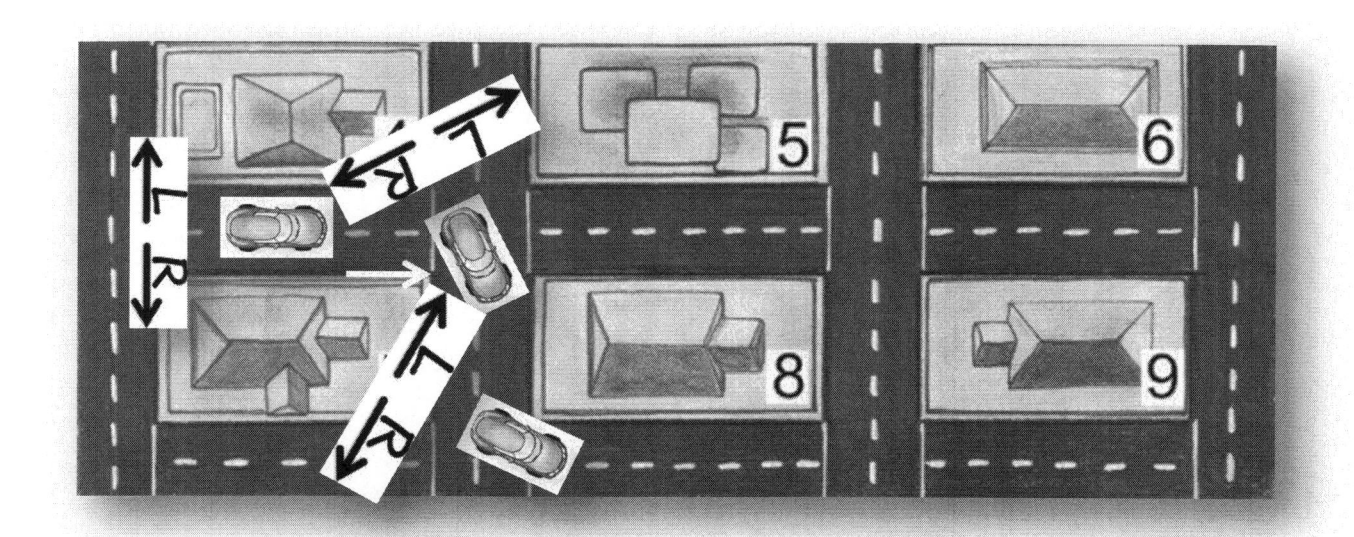

the **left/right marker** is positioned *behind* the vehicle at all times.

Working Memory – Street Directions

Intermediate Level

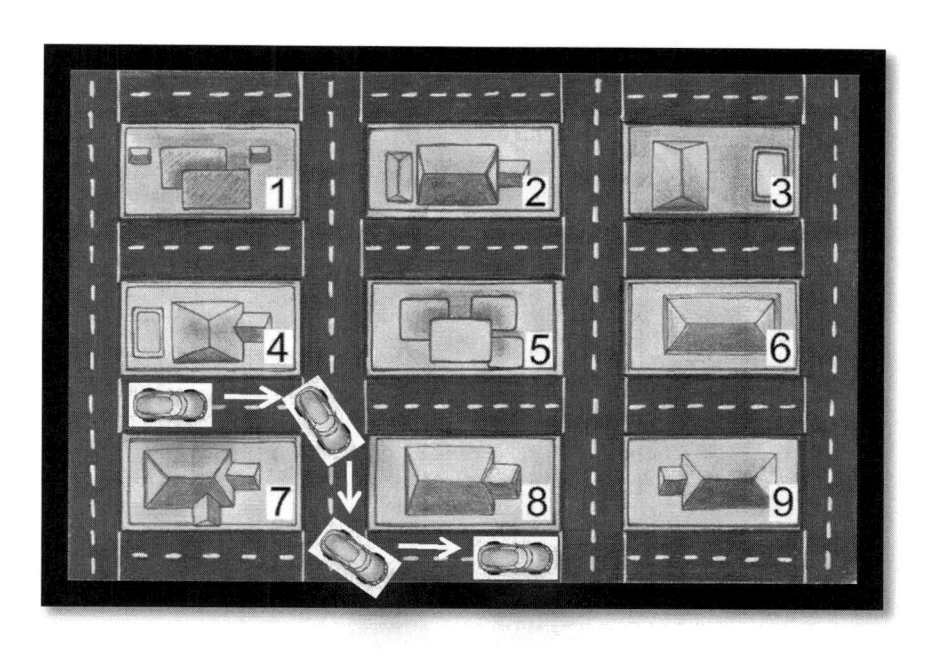

Activity 1

1. Place the car between and to the left of buildings 4 and 7 pointing *east*, then move to the end of the street and stop.
2. Turn right onto the highway and go forward 50 meters.
3. Turn left into the street and then stop at the end of the street.

(You should be at the bottom of building 8 pointing east)

Working Memory Activities

Working Memory – Street Directions

Intermediate Level

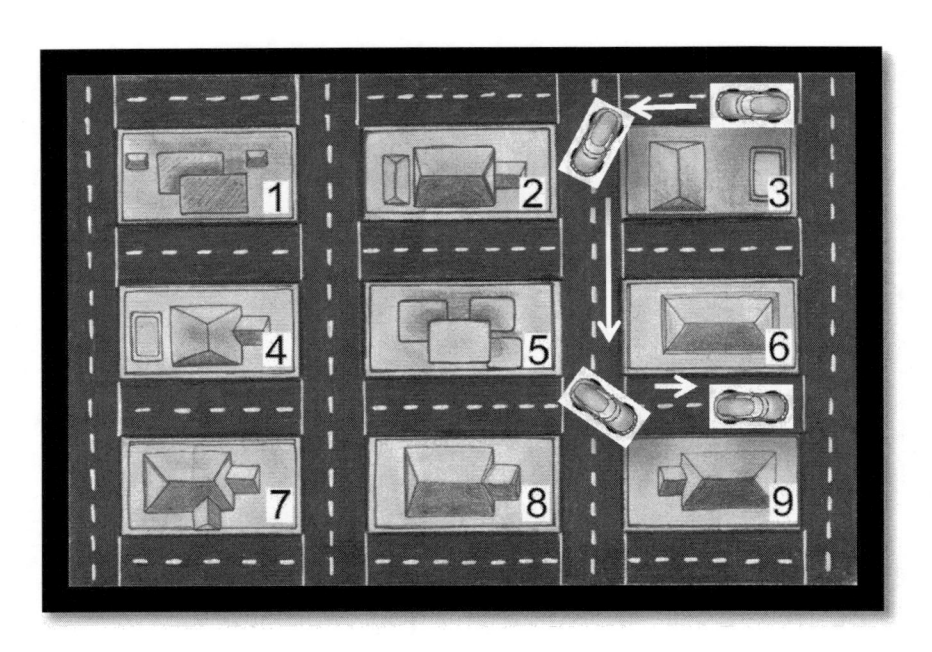

Activity 2

1. Place the car above and to the right of building 3 pointing *west*, then move to the end of the street and stop.
2. Turn left onto the highway and go forward 100 meters.
3. Turn left into the street, move forward to the end of the street and stop.

(You should be between buildings 6 and 9 pointing east)

Street Directions

Working Memory – Street Directions

Intermediate Level

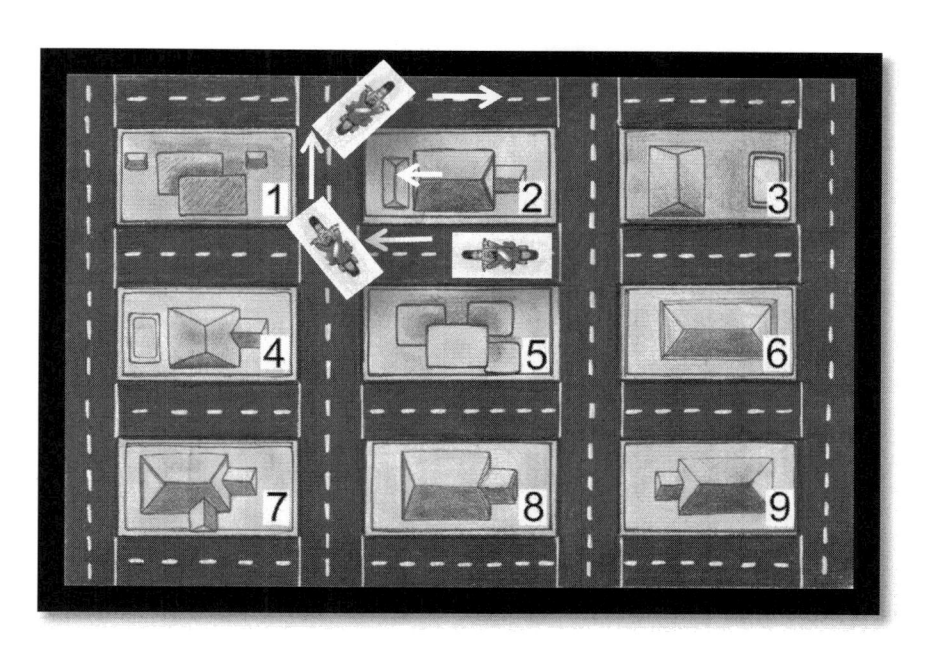

Activity 3

1. Place the motorbike between and to the right of buildings 2 and 5 pointing *west*, then move to the end of the street.
2. Turn right onto the highway and go forward 50 meters.
3. Turn right into the street and stop at the end of the street.

(You should be above and to the right of building 2 pointing east)

Working Memory – Street Directions

Intermediate Level

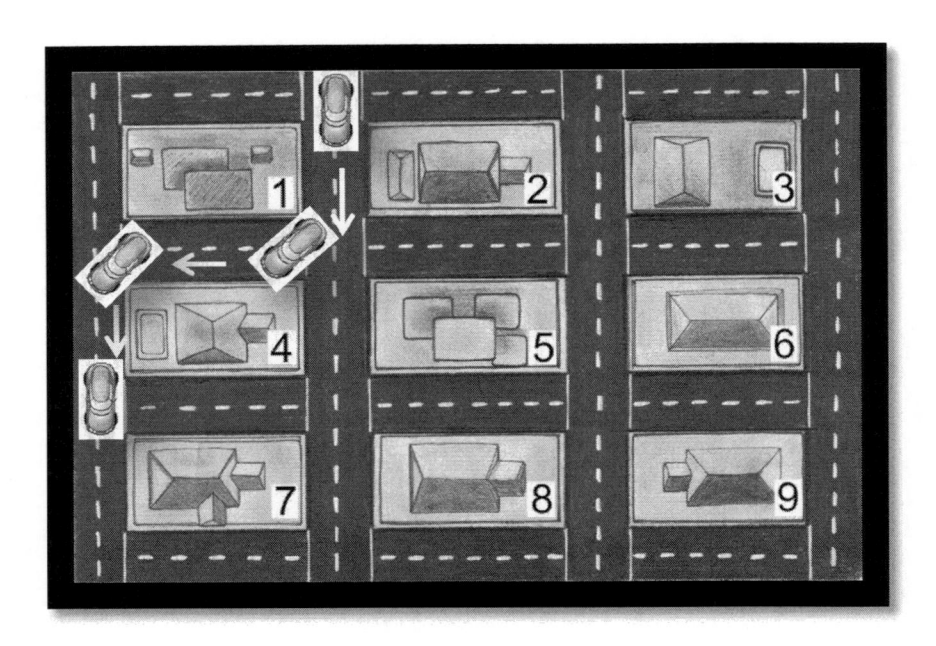

Activity 4

1. Place the car above and between buildings 1 and 2 pointing *south, then* go forward 50 meters.
2. Turn right into the street and then stop at the end of the street.
3. Turn left onto the highway and go forward 50 meters.

(You should be on the highway between and to the left of buildings 4 and 7 pointing south)

Working Memory – Street Directions

Intermediate Level

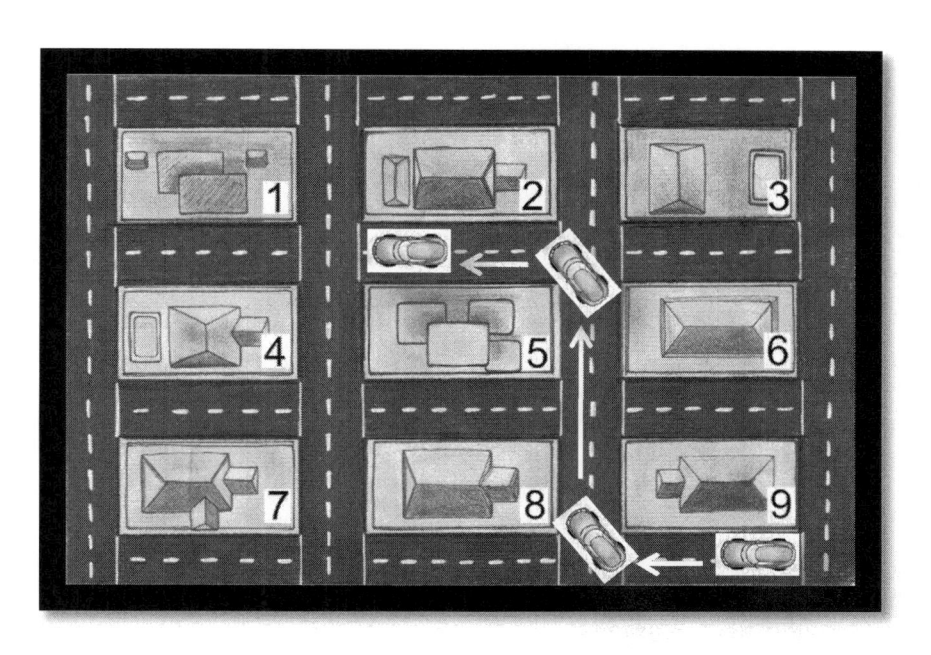

Activity 5

1. Place the car on the street below and to the right of building 9 pointing *west*, then move to the end of the street.
2. Turn right onto the highway and travel 100 meters.
3. Turn left into the street and stop at the end of the street.

   (You should be between and to the left of buildings 2 and 5 pointing west)

Working Memory Activities

Working Memory – Street Directions

Intermediate Level

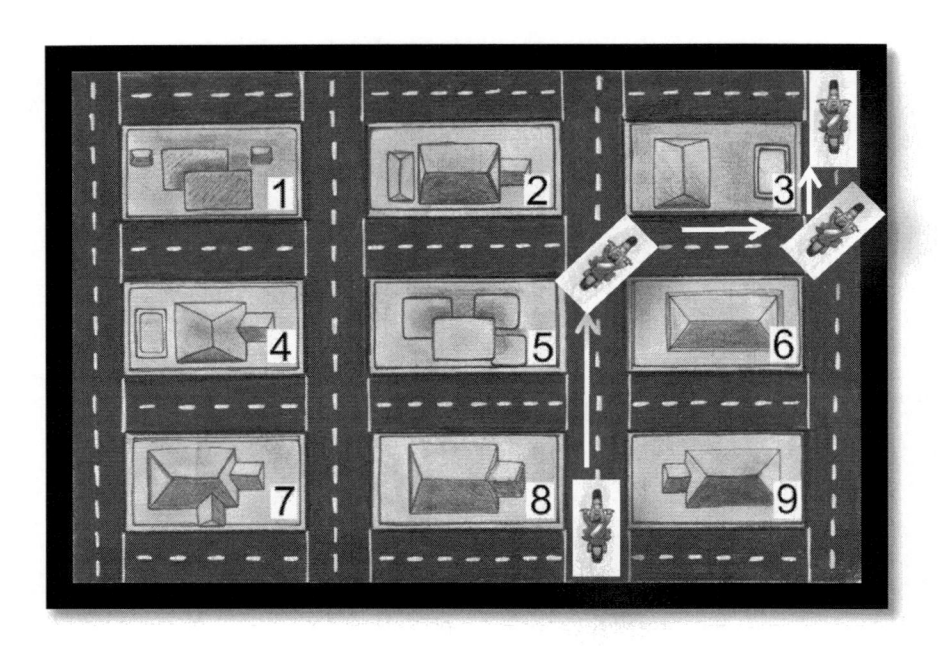

Activity 6

1. Place the motorbike between and at the bottom of buildings 8 and 9 pointing *north*, then travel 100 meters.
2. Turn right into the street and go to the end of the street.
3. Turn left onto the highway and travel 50 meters.

(You should be above and to the right of building 3 pointing north)

Working Memory – Street Directions

Intermediate Level

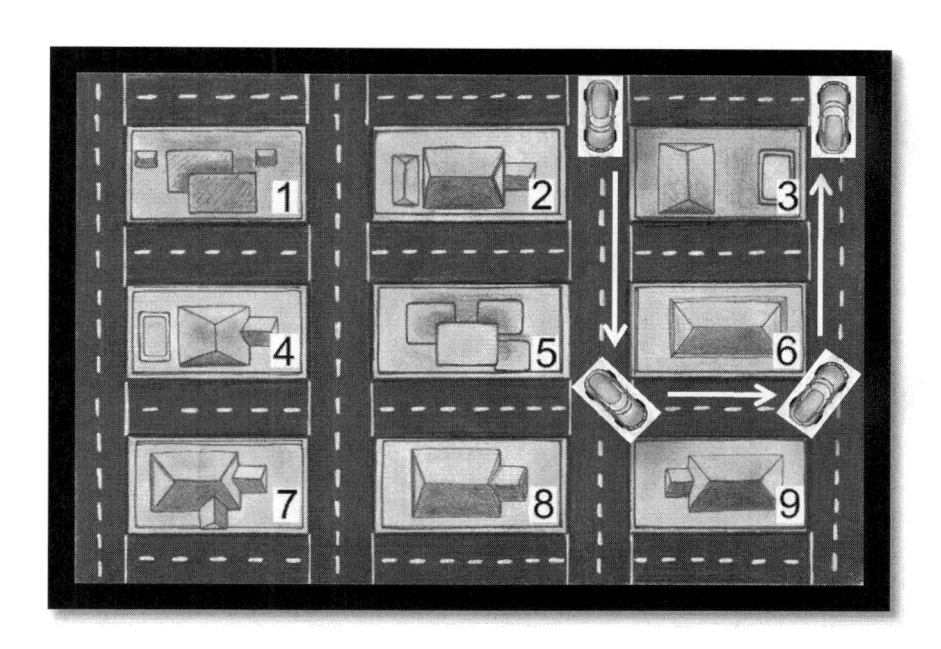

Activity 7

1. Place the car above and between buildings 2 and 3 pointing *south* and then travel forward 100 meters.
2. Turn left into the street and stop at the end of the street.
3. Turn left onto the highway and go forward 100 meters.

   (You should be on the highway above and to the right of building 3 pointing north)

Working Memory – Street Directions

Intermediate Level

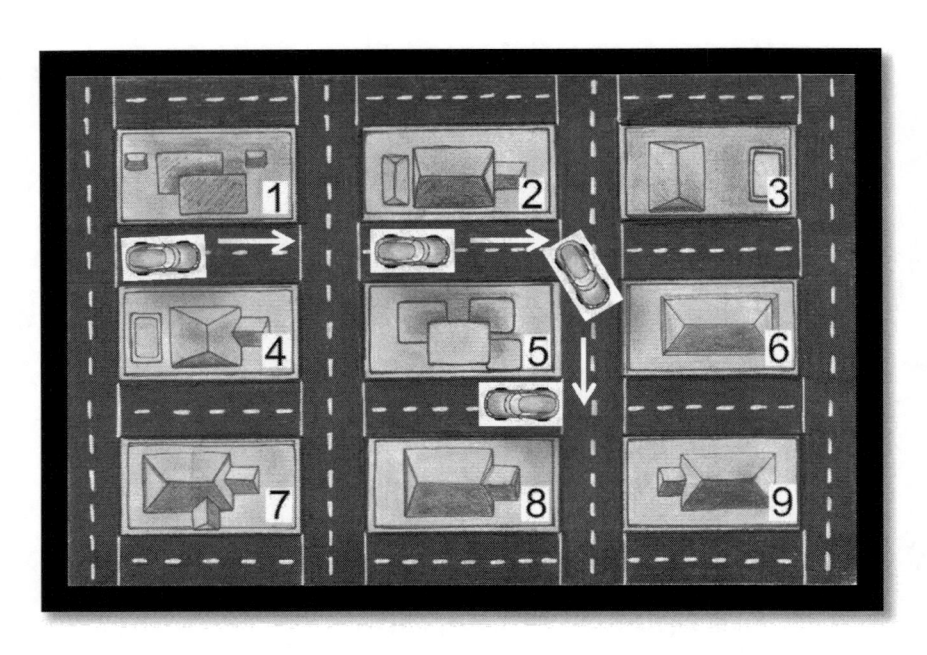

Activity 8

1. Place the car to the left and between buildings 1 and 4 pointing *east*, then drive to the end of the street and stop.
2. Cross the highway and then drive to the end of the street.
3. Turn right onto the highway, move forward 50 meters, then turn right again and stop.

(You should be to the right and between buildings 5 and 8 pointing west)

Working Memory – Street Directions

Intermediate Level

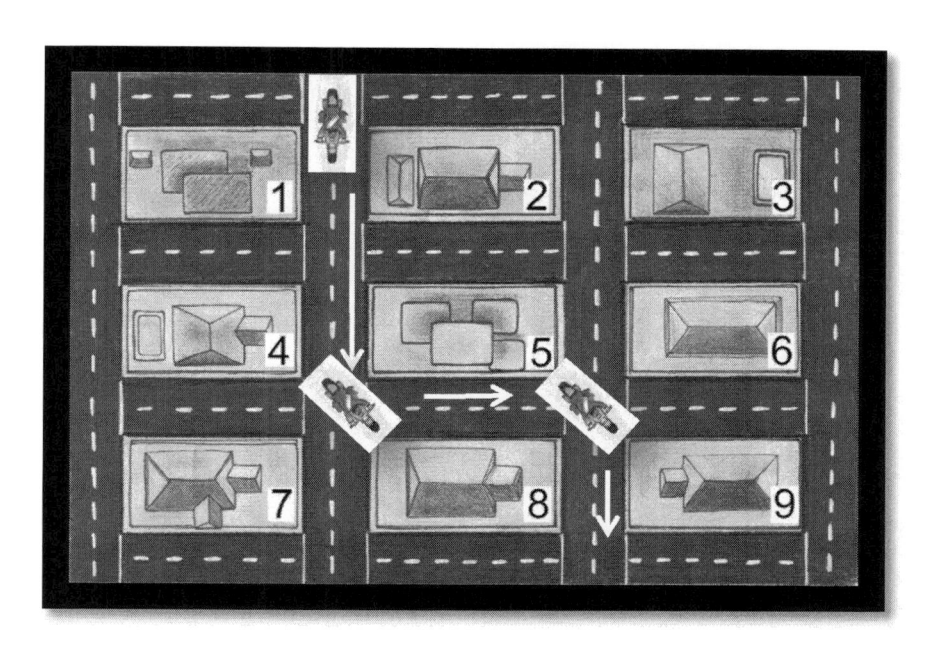

Activity 9

1. Place the motorbike above and between buildings 1 and 2 pointing *south,* then travel 100 meters.
2. Turn left into the street and stop at the end of the street.
3. Turn right onto the highway and travel 50 meters.

   (You should be below and between buildings 8 and 9 pointing south)

Working Memory – Street Directions

Intermediate Level

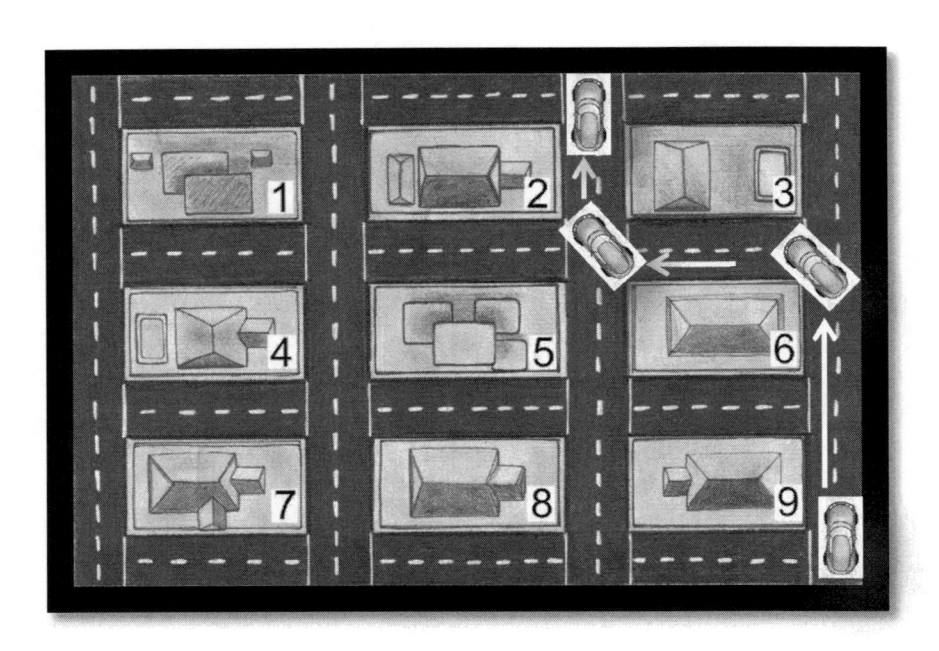

Activity 10

1. Place the car to the right and below building 9, pointing *north*, then move forward 100 meters.

2. Turn left into the street and drive to the end of the street.

3. Turn right onto the highway, move forward 50 meters and then stop.

   (You should be above and between buildings 1 and 2 pointing north)

Working Memory – Street Directions

Record Sheet

Tick √ for correct and ✗ for incorrect

Intermediate Level

1. Activity __ __ __

2. Activty __ __ __

3. Activity __ __ __

4. Activity __ __ __

5. Activity __ __ __

6. Activity __ __ __

7. Activity __ __ __

8. Activity __ __ __

9. Activity __ __ __

10. Activity __ __ __

Working Memory – Street Directions

Advanced Level

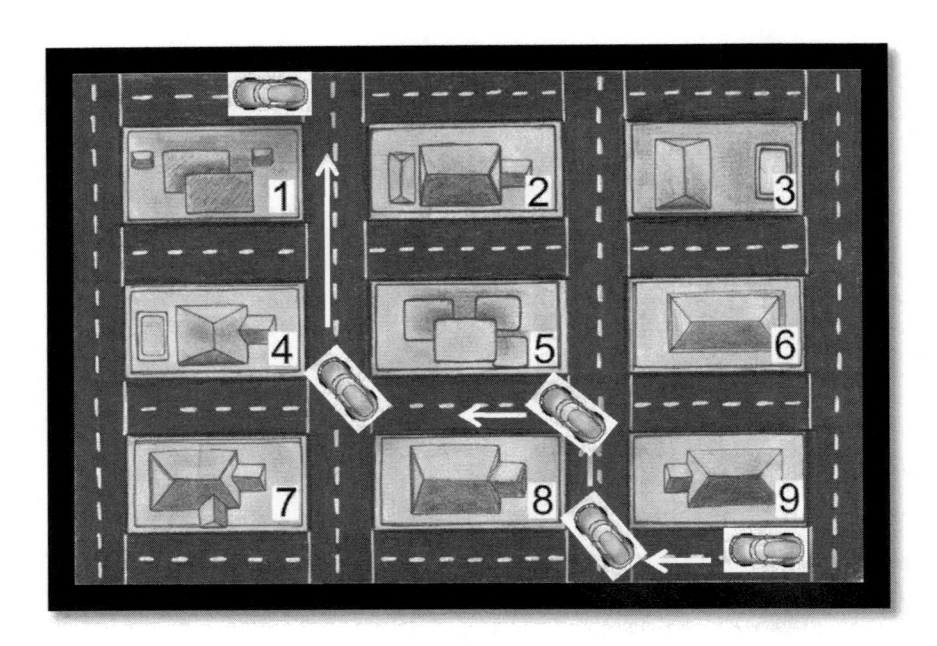

Activity 1

1. Place the car below and to the right of building 9 pointing *west*, then move to the end of the street.
2. Turn right onto the highway and travel 50 meters.
3. Turn left into the street and stop at the end of the street.
4. Turn right onto the highway, travel 100 meters and then turn left into the street.

(You should be above and building 1 pointing west)

Working Memory – Street Directions

Advanced Level

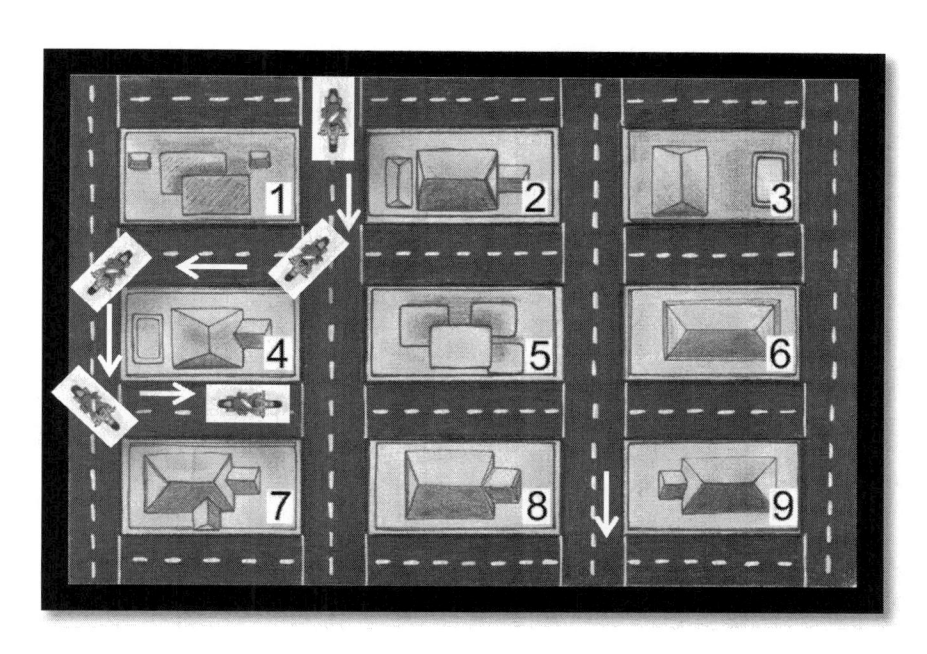

Activity 2

1. Place the motorbike above and between buildings 1 and 2 pointing *south*, then travel 50 meters.
2. Turn right into the street then stop at the end of the street.
3. Turn left onto the highway and travel 50 meters.
4. Turn left into the street and stop at the end of the street.

   (You should be between and to the right of buildings 4 and 7 pointing east)

Working Memory Activities

Working Memory – Street Directions

Advanced Level

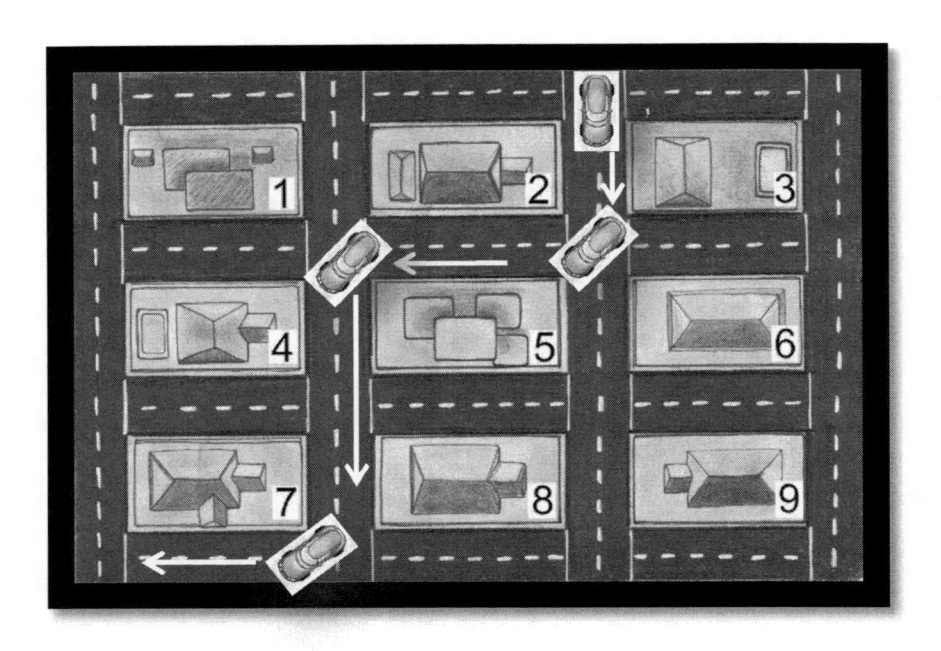

Activity 3

1. Place the car above and between buildings 2 and 3 pointing *south,* then travel forward 50 meters.
2. Turn right into the street and then stop at the end of the street.
3. Turn left onto the highway and go forward 100 meters.
4. Turn right into the street and stop at the end of the street.

   (You should be below and to the left of building7 pointing west.)

Working Memory – Street Directions

Advanced Level

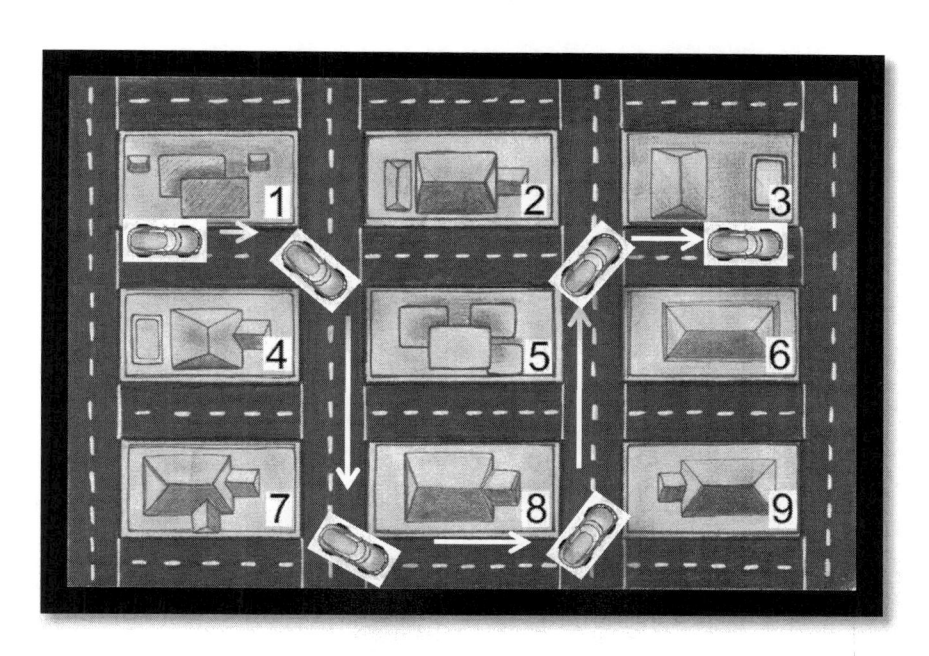

Activity 4

1. Place the car to the left and between buildings 1 and 4 pointing *east*, then go to the end of the street and turn right.
2. Move 100 meters and then turn left into the street.
3. Move to the end of the street and then turn left.
4. Go 100 meters, turn right into the street and stop at the end of the street.

(You should be to the right and between buildings 3 and 6.)

Working Memory – Street Directions

Advanced Level

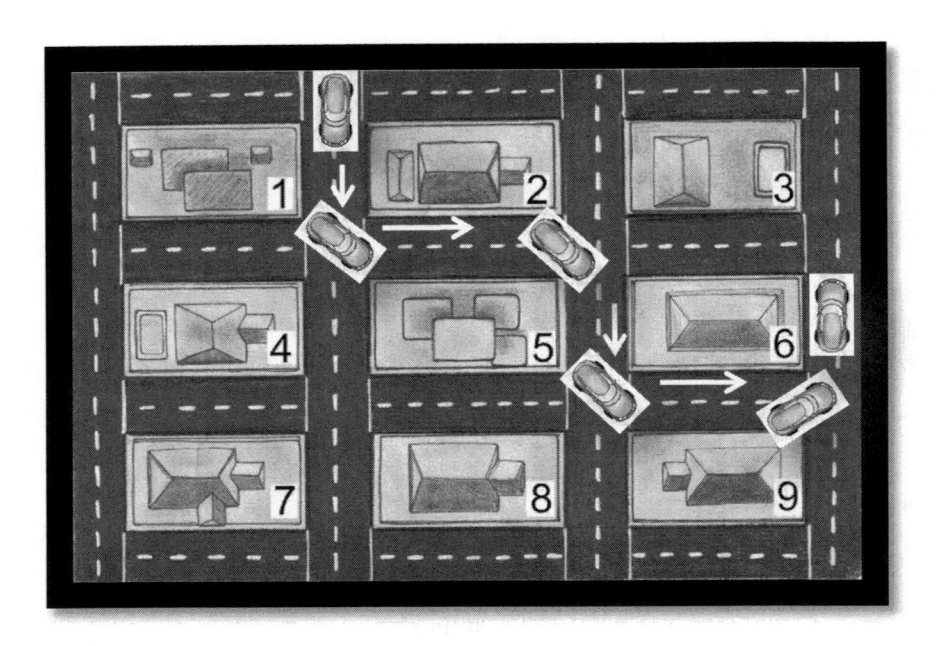

Activity 5

1. Place the car above and between buildings 1 and 2 pointing *south*, then go forward 50 meters.
2. Turn left, go the end of the street and then turn right.
3. Go forward 50 meters and then turn left into the street.
4. Go to the end of the street and then turn left onto the highway.

(You should be beside building 6 pointing north)

Street Directions

Working Memory – Street Directions

Advanced Level

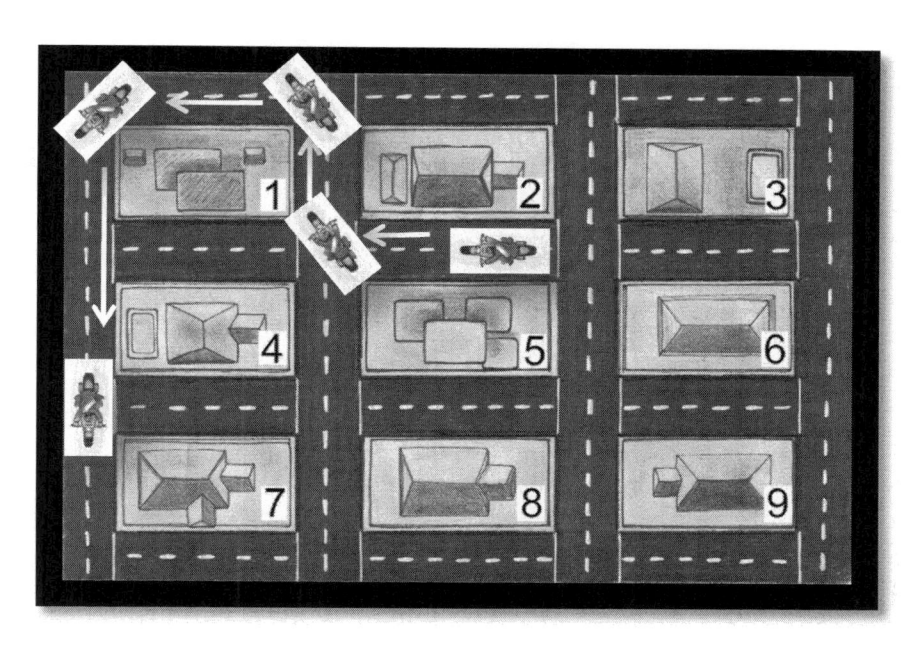

Activity 6

1. Place the motorbike between and to the right of buildings 2 and 5 pointing *west*, then move to the end of the street.
2. Turn right onto the highway and go forward 50 meters.
3. Turn left into the street then stop at the end of the street.
4. Turn left onto the highway and go forward 100 meters.

(You should be on the highway to the left of buildings 4 and 7 pointing south)

Working Memory Activities

Working Memory – Street Directions

Advanced Level

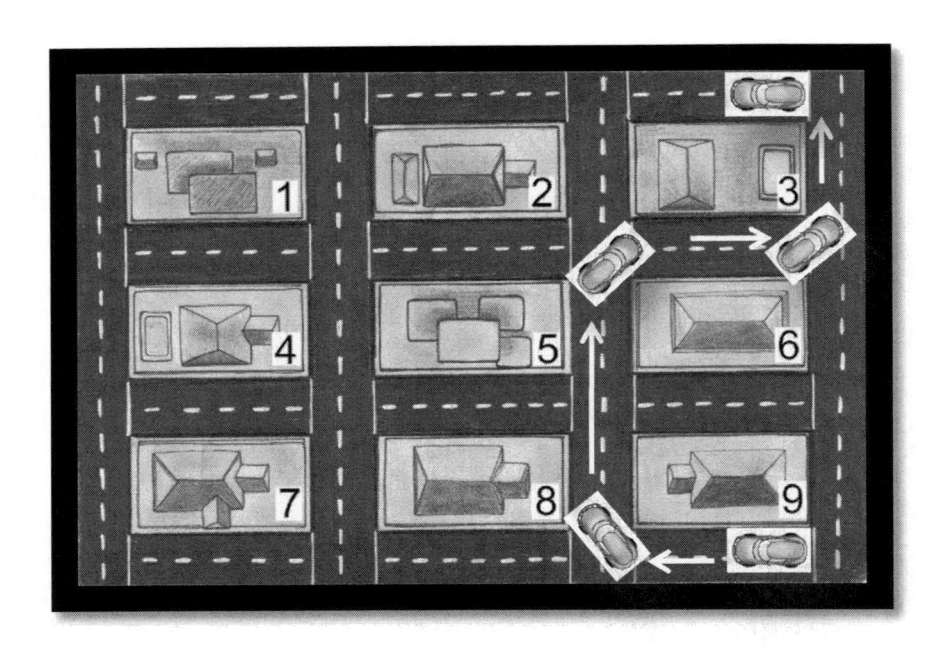

Activity 7

1. Place the car below and to the right of building 9 pointing *west* then move to the end of the street.

2. Turn right onto the highway and travel 100 meters.

3. Turn right into the street, stop at the end and then turn left.

4. Go 50 meters on the highway and then turn left.

(You should be above and to the right of building 3 pointing west)

Street Directions

Working Memory – Street Directions

Advanced Level

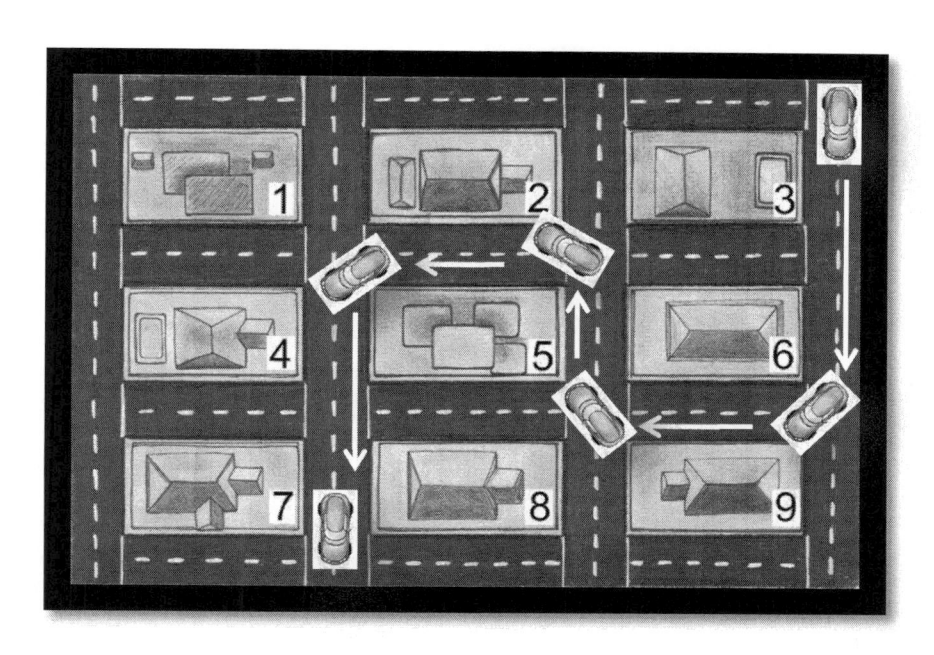

Activity 8

1. Place the car on the highway above and to the right of building 3 pointing *south*, then travel 100 meters.

2. Turn right into the street, go forward to the end of the street and then turn right onto the highway.

3. Go forward 50 meters, turn left, and then stop at street's end.

4. Turn left onto the highway and go forward 100 meters.

(You should be between buildings 7 and 8, pointing south)

Working Memory – Street Directions

Advanced Level

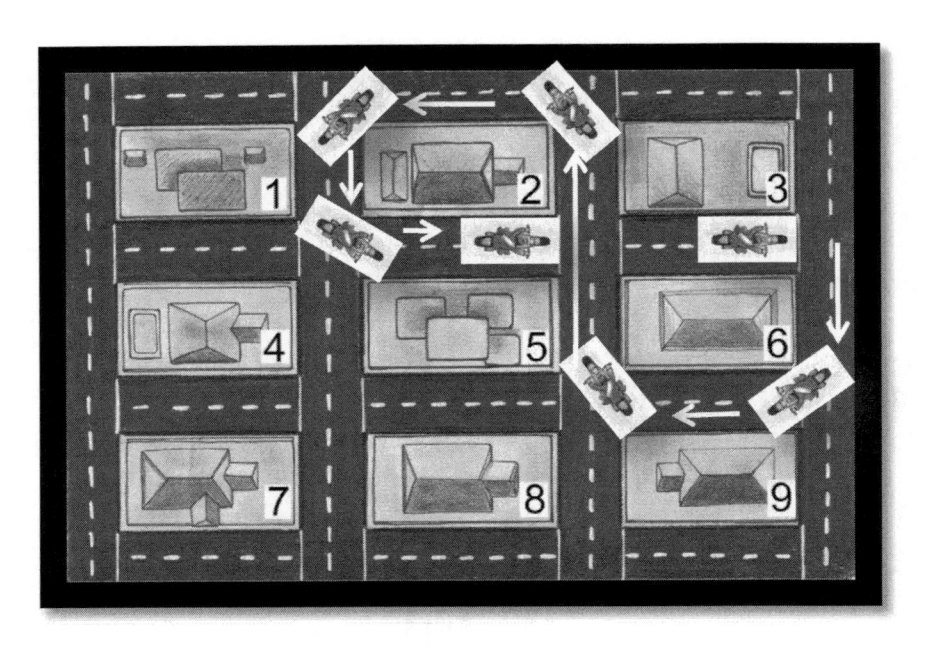

Activity 9

1. Place the motorbike between and to the right of buildings 3 and 6, pointing *east*, then turn right onto the highway.
2. Go 50 meters, turn right, go to the end then turn right.
3. Go 100 meters, turn left, go to the end then turn left.
4. Go 50 meters, turn left, go the end of the street and stop.

(You should be between and to the right of buildings 2 and 5 pointing east)

Street Directions

Working Memory – Street Directions

Advanced Level

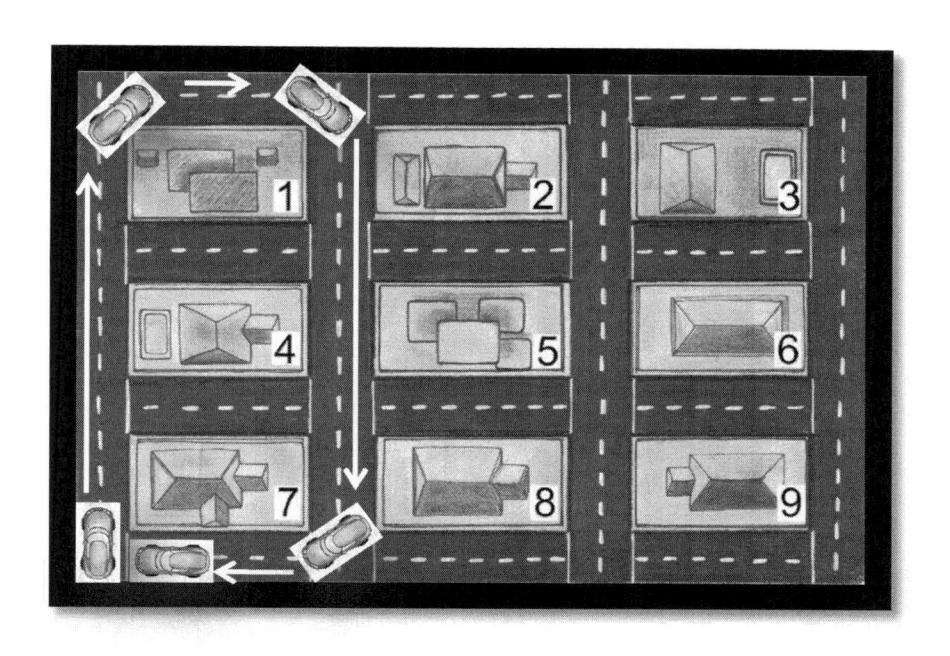

Activity 10

1. Place the car below and to the left of building 7 on the highway pointing *north,* then go forward 150 meters.

2. Turn right, go to the end of the street, then turn right onto the highway.

3. Go forward 150 meters and then turn right,

4. Go to the end of the street and then turn right onto the highway.

   (You should be back where you started)

Working Memory – Street Directions

Record Sheet

Tick √ for correct and ✗ for incorrect

Advanced Level

1. Activity __ __ __ __

2. Activty __ __ __ __

3. Activity __ __ __ __

4. Activity __ __ __ __

5. Activity __ __ __ __

6. Activity __ __ __ __

7. Activity __ __ __ __

8. Activity __ __ __ __

9. Activity __ __ __ __

10. Activity __ __ __ __

References

Alloway, T.P. (2010) Improving Working Memory: Supporting Students' Learning, *Sage Publications, Ltd*

Alloway, T.P. (2007) Automated Working Memory Assessment. *Harcourt Education: London*

Boudreau, D. & Costanza-Smith, A. (2011) Assessment and Treatment of Working Memory Deficits in School-Age Children: The Role of the Speech-Language Pathologist. *Language, Speech and Hearing Services in Schools,* Vol 42, 152-166.

Gathercole, S.E. & Alloway, T.P. (2008) Working Memory and Learning: A Practical Guide for Teachers *Sage Publications, Ltd*

Smith, C.G. (2008) Verbal Working Memory and Storytelling in School-Age Children with Autism, *Language, Speech and Hearing Services in Schools, Vol 39, 498-511.*

Wagner, R.K Muse, A.E & Tannenbaum, K.R. (2007) Vocabulary Acquisition: Implications for Reading Comprehension. *The Guilford Press*

Appendix A

Activity Items

As an option, **Appendix A** is available to print and download from speechlanguage-resources.com. The **Working Memory Activities** book is perfect bound which can make photocopying a little tricky at times. So the download option is for those who don't wish to stretch the book's binding. **Appendix A** can be found on this web address:

http://www.speechlanguage-resources.com/wm-ex-app.html

You will need to *type* the above code directly into your internet browser's **address bar**.

Do not type the code into the search engine box, but the address bar, which is located close to the top of the browser. On the webpage you will be able to download and print the **Appendix A** activities and playing boards.

Photocopiable

Memory Test – Part 1

Student Name: _____   Date of Birth: _____

Date: *Pre-Test*: _____   Date: *Post-Test:* _____

Instructions: I am going to read a short sequence of numbers. You have to repeat the numbers back to me. So if I say 7 3, you say 7 3. I can only say the numbers once, so listen carefully.

Part 1 – Digits *Forwards*

Digits:	Pre-test	Post-test
4 8	_____	_____
6 3	_____	_____
9 7	_____	_____
8 5	_____	_____

Digits:	Pre-test	Post-test
6 9 2	_____	_____
4 7 3	_____	_____
9 5 1	_____	_____
8 3 9	_____	_____

Digits:	Pre-test	Post-test
6 1 4 5	_____	_____
4 3 8 1	_____	_____
9 8 1 4	_____	_____
8 7 1 9	_____	_____

Digits:	Pre-test	Post-test
9 3 1 8 7	_____	_____
1 7 2 4 8	_____	_____
6 3 1 2 1	_____	_____
1 3 9 6 8	_____	_____

Photocopiable

Memory Test – Part 2

Instructions: I am going to read a short sequence of numbers. You have to repeat the numbers back to me, but this time it's a little different. I want you to say the numbers *backwards*. So if I say 7 3, you say 3 7. I can only say the numbers once, so listen carefully.

Part 2 – Digits *Backwards*

Digits:		Pre-test	Post-test
3 9	(9 3)	_____	_____
6 3	(3 6)	_____	_____
9 7	(7 9)	_____	_____
8 5	(5 8)	_____	_____

Digits:		Pre-test	Post-test
2 9 4	(4 9 2)	_____	_____
4 7 3	(3 7 4)	_____	_____
8 5 4	(4 5 8)	_____	_____
7 3 1	(1 3 7)	_____	_____

Digits:		Pre-test	Post-test
9 1 2 8	(8 2 1 9)	_____	_____
4 1 5 9	(9 5 1 4)	_____	_____
3 7 1 2	(2 1 7 3)	_____	_____
2 8 7 1	(1 7 8 2)	_____	_____

Digits:		Pre-test	Post-test
6 3 1 8 1	(1 8 1 3 6)	_____	_____
7 3 2 4 9	(9 4 2 3 7)	_____	_____
1 3 4 2 7	(7 2 4 3 1)	_____	_____
4 3 7 6 2	(2 6 7 3 4)	_____	_____

Colours – House Drawing *Photocopiable*

Colours – Farm Animals Drawing *Photocopiable*

171

Colours – Train and Carriage Drawing
Photocopiable

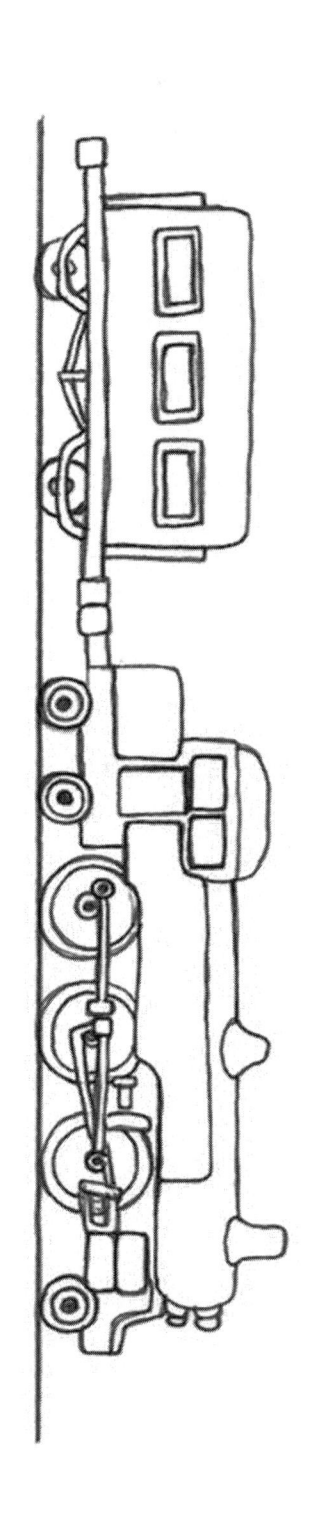

Home Furniture - House Plan *Photocopiable*

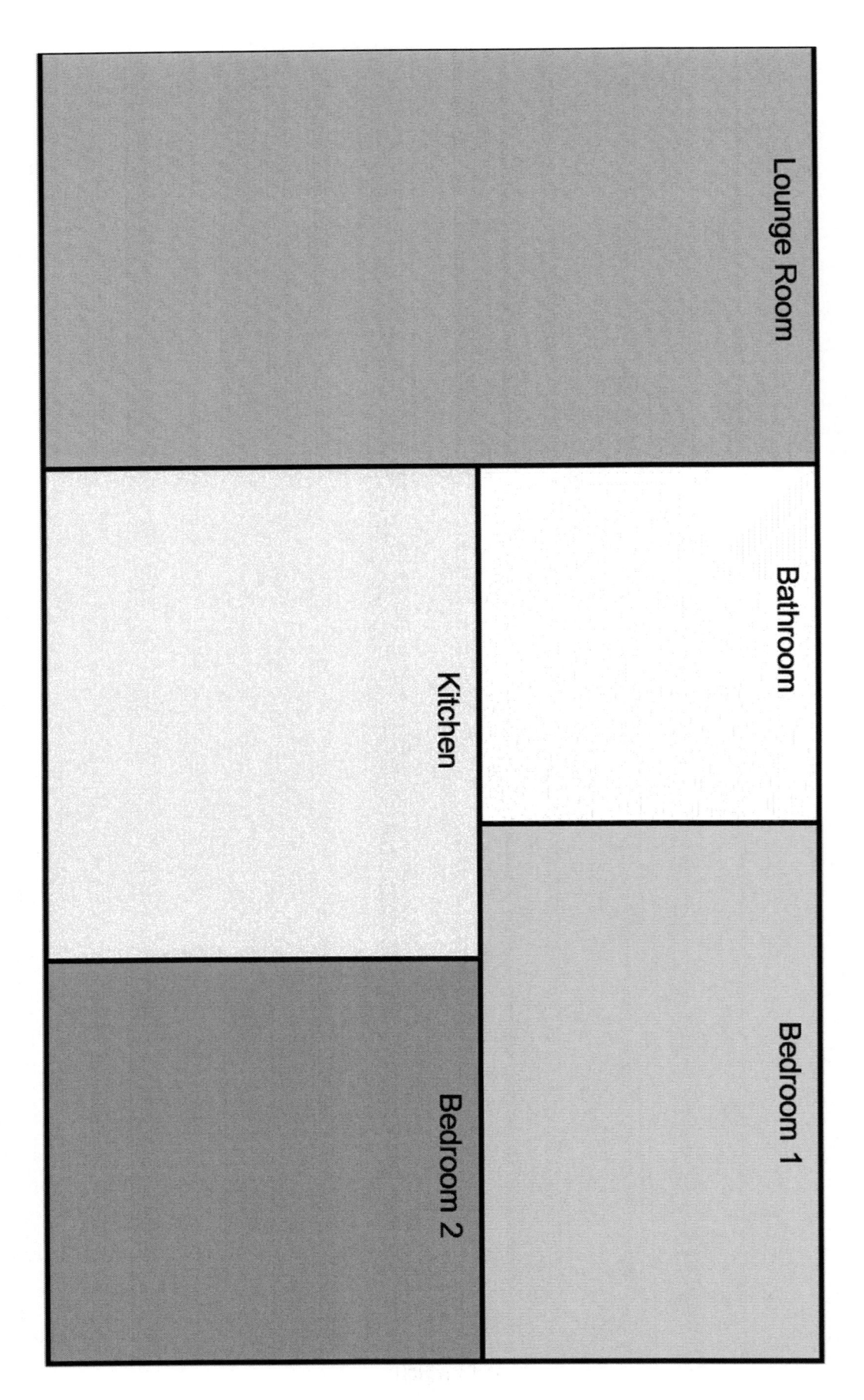

Lounge Room	
Kitchen	Bathroom
Bedroom 2	Bedroom 1

Home Furniture – Furniture Items *Photocopiable*

- Two Seat Sofa
- Bath Tub
- Striped Bed
- Dining Table
- Bookshelf
- Three Seat Sofa
- Toilet
- Shower
- Bathroom Vanity
- Kitchen Table
- Chair
- Fridge
- Cooktop
- Kitchen Sink
- Plain Bed
- Side Table

Shapes Box *Photocopiable*

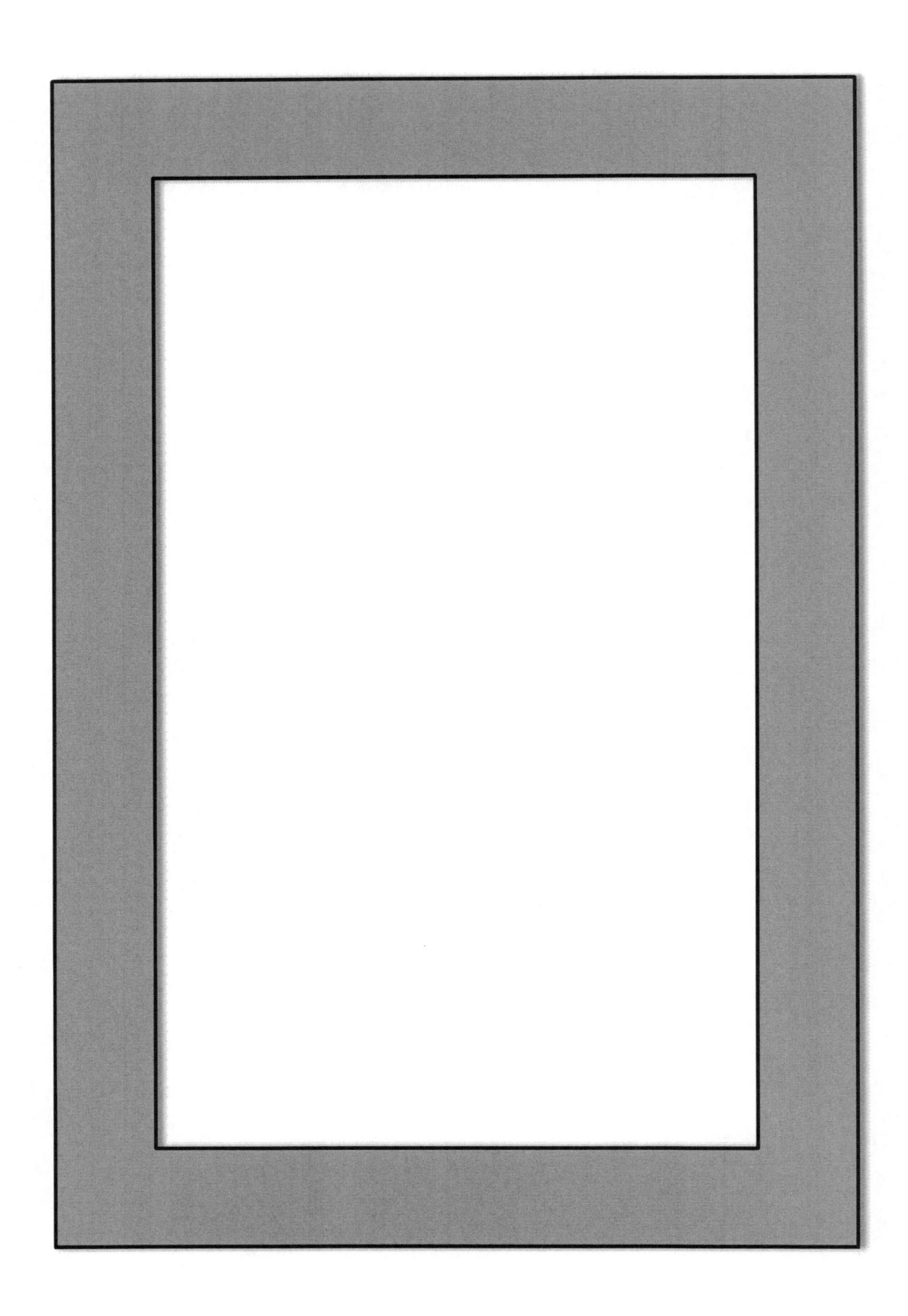

Working Memory Shapes

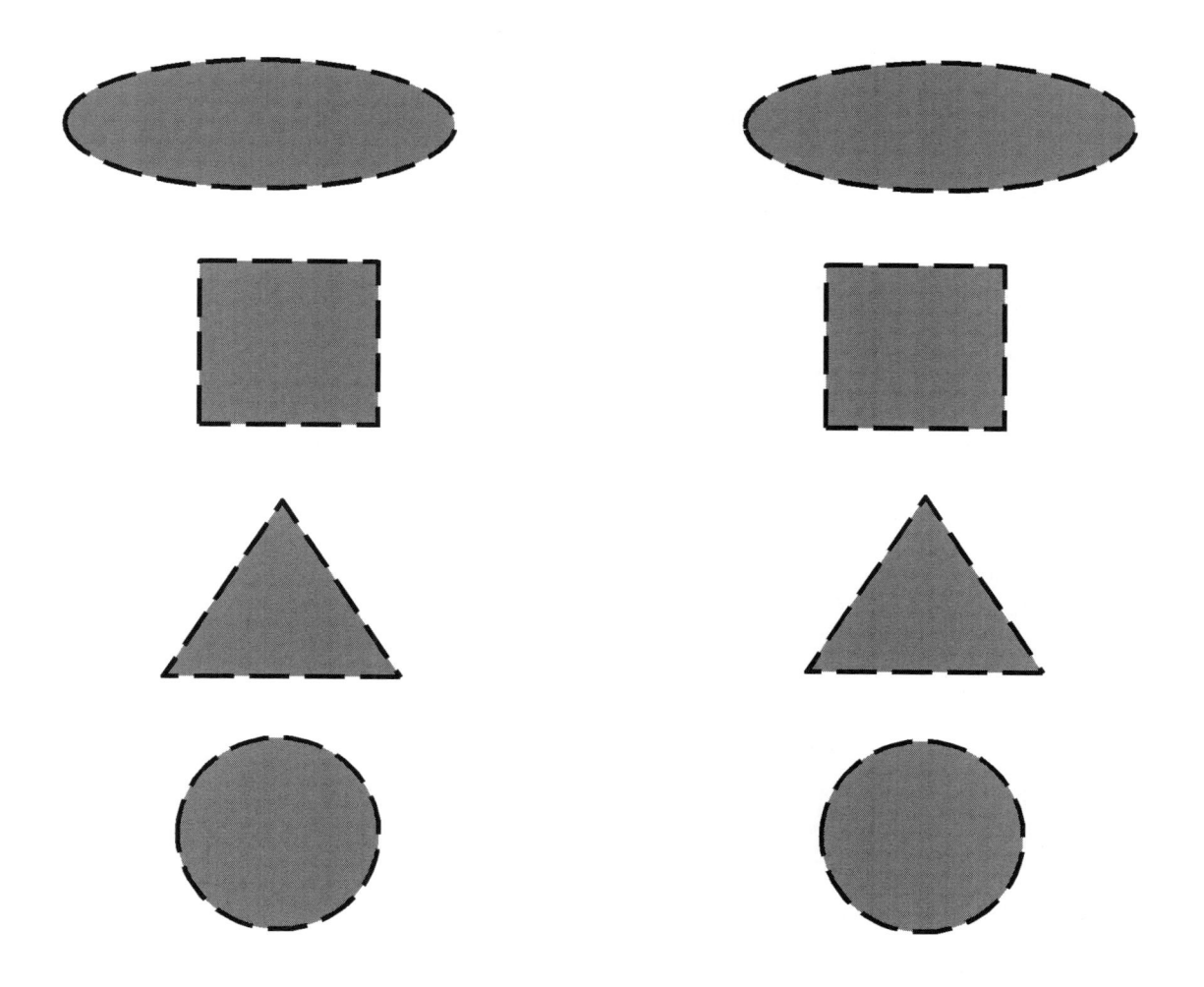

Street Directions – Game Items

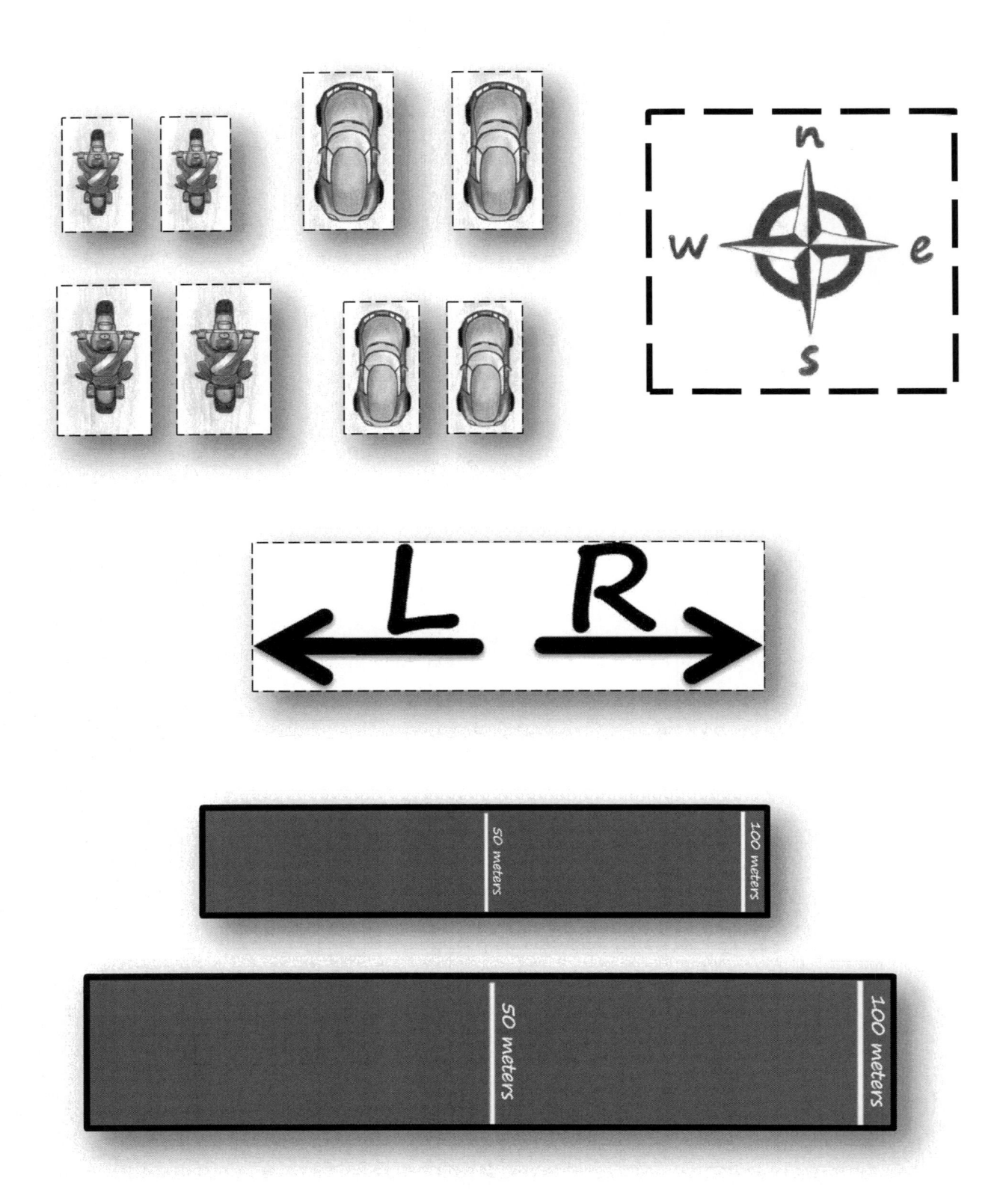

177

Street Directions Map

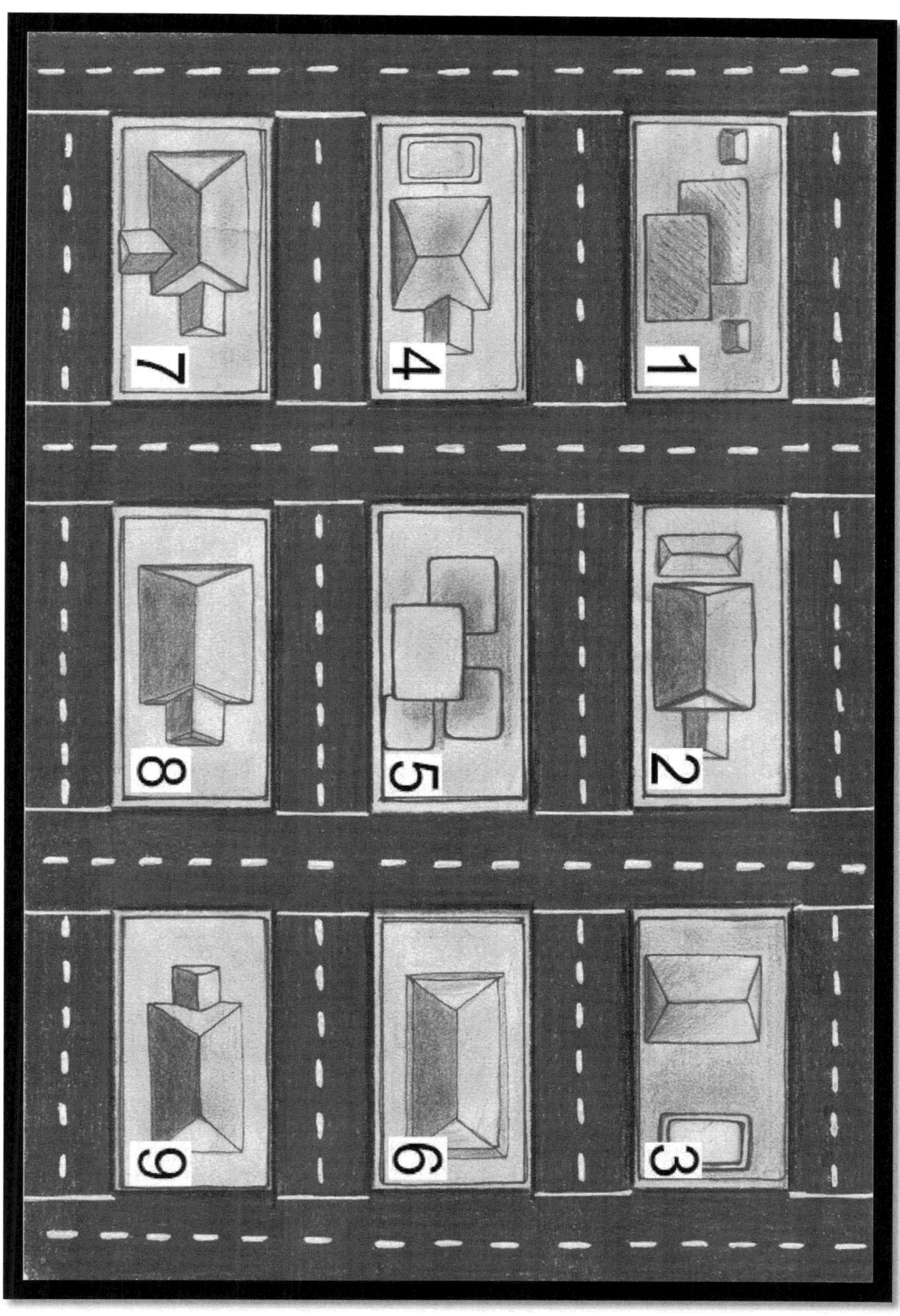

Appendix B

Answer Section

Answer Section

Smallest to Largest

a. mouse – cat – cow   b. dog – sheep – cow   c. chicken – goat - horse

d. flea – ladybug – moth   e. ant - ladybug – goliath beetle   f. midge – ant – wasp   g. starling – eagle - ostrich   h. hummingbird – swan - emu   i. finch – duck – albatross   j. meerkat – leopard – rhinoceros   k. meerkat – hyena – giraffe   l. mongoose – warthog - buffalo

Smallest to Largest

a. cherry – orange - grapefruit   b. grape – apple - watermelon   c. plum – lemon - watermelon   d. bean – zucchini - cabbage   e. bean – capsicum - pumpkin   f. peas – sweet potato - eggplant   g. peanut – macadamia nut – brazil nut   h. sesame seed – almond - chestnut   i. pumpkin seed – peanut - walnut

Longest to Shortest

a. ruler – pen - finger   b. train – truck - motorbike   c. baseball bat – spanner – paper clip   d. tree – branch - twig   e. river – lake – pond   f. shark barracouta – sardine

Shortest to Tallest

Chihuahua – Spaniel – St Bernard b. Pygmy monkey – Baboon – Gorilla c. Meerkat – Lion – Giraffe d. hillock – hill – mountain e. dollhouse – shed – skyscraper f. flower weed – shrub - tree

Heaviest to Lightest

a. medicine ball – football – tennis ball b. basketball – baseball – golf ball c. street sweeper – broom - toothbrush d. aircraft carrier – motorboat – dinghy e. truck – motorbike – scooter f. passenger jet – helicopter – ultra light g. hawk – moth – flea h. elephant - dog – mouse i. ostrich – hawk – canary j. flat screen TV – laptop – watch k. computer – book – pen l. oven – frypan - glass

Thickest to Thinnest

a. brick – sausage - pin b. encyclopaedia – newspaper - card c. cable – rope – thread d. log – bean - pin e. leg – finger – single hair f. tree trunk – branch - pin g. hippopotamus – goat – praying mantis h. car tire – cake – dinner plate i. loaf of bread – CD cover – paper j. rocket s hip – harpoon – arrow k. tree - nail – pin l. car tire – cake - DVD

Coldest to Warmest

a. snow – rainforest - desert b. Antarctica – Sahara – beach in Australia c. Winter – Autumn/Fall – Summer d. ice-cube – apple – hot chocolate e. frozen peas – apple – hot pie f. icy pole – honey – hot soup g. snow field – hall – hot tub h. snowfield forest – erupting volcano i. water from fridge – tap water – hot chocolate j. Arctic ocean – lake – hot springs k. snow desert sand lava l. tap water – hot springs - lava

About the Author

David Newman is speech-language pathologist and sometime writer who lives and works in Victoria, Australia.

David self publishes books and workbooks to help school-age children acquire language and literacy skills. Starting from scratch, David has created a website - speech-language-resources.com - that has dozens of user-friendly webpages and a wealth of free programs, games and guides to assist teachers, parents and speech-language pathologists improve children's language skills.

David is a full-time speech-language pathologist working in Victorian schools. He writes workbooks mostly in his spare time often curled up on the couch cradling a laptop huddled near a gas heater sipping cups of hot tea while listening to music on headphones.

www.speechlanguage-resources.com

Printed in Great Britain
by Amazon